easy learning

Greek

phrasebook

Consultant
Maria Koutsoubou

First published 1993
This edition published 2010
Copyright © HarperCollins Publishers
Reprint 10 9 8 7 6 5 4 3 2 1
Typeset by Davidson Pre-Press, Glasgow
Printed in Italy by L.E.G.O. S.p.A., Lavis (Trento)

www.collinslanguage.com

ISBN 978-0-00-735852-6

Using your phrasebook

Your *Collins Gem Phrasebook* is designed to help you locate the exact phrase you need, when you need it, whether on holiday or for business. If you want to adapt the phrases, you can easily see where to substitute your own words using the dictionary section, and the clear, full-colour layout gives you direct access to the different topics.

The Gem Phrasebook includes:

- Over 70 topics arranged thematically. Each phrase is accompanied by a simple pronunciation guide which eliminates any problems pronouncing foreign words.

- A Top ten tips section to safeguard against any cultural faux pas, giving essential dos and don'ts for situations involving local customs or etiquette.

- Practical hints to make your stay trouble free, showing you where to go and what to do when dealing with everyday matters such as travel or hotels and offering valuable tourist information.

- Face to face sections so that you understand what is being said to you. These example mini-dialogues give you a good idea of what to expect from a real conversation.

- Common announcements and messages you may hear, ensuring that you never miss the important information you need to know when out and about.

- A clearly laid-out 3000-word dictionary means you will never be stuck for words.

- A basic grammar section which will enable you to build on your phrases.

- A list of public holidays to avoid being caught out by unexpected opening and closing hours, and to make sure you don't miss the celebrations!

It's worth spending time before you embark on your travels just looking through the topics to see what is covered and becoming familiar with what might be said to you.

Whatever the situation, your *Gem Phrasebook* is sure to help!

Contents

Using your		Petrol	48
phrasebook	3	Breakdown	49
Pronouncing Greek	7	Car parts	50
Top ten tips	10	Road signs	52
Talking to people	13	**Staying somewhere**	54
Hello/goodbye, yes/no	13	Hotel (booking)	54
Key phrases	15	Hotel (desk)	57
Signs and notices	19	Hotel (room service)	58
Polite expressions	21	Camping	59
Celebrations	22	Self-catering	61
Making friends	23	**Shopping**	62
Work	25	Shopping phrases	62
Weather	26	Shops	64
Getting around	27	Food (general)	64
Asking the way	27	Food (fruit and veg)	65
Bus and coach	30	Clothes	67
Metro	32	Clothes (articles)	68
Train	34	Maps and guides	69
Taxi	37	Post office	70
Boat and ferry	38	Photos	71
Air travel	40	**Leisure**	72
Customs control	42	Sightseeing and	
Driving	43	tourist office	72
Car hire	43	Entertainment	74
Motorbike hire	45	Leisure/interests	75
Driving	47	Music	76

Beach	77
Theatre/opera	78
Television	79
Sport	80
Walking	81
Communications	82
Telephone and mobile	82
E-mail	85
Internet	86
Fax	87
Practicalities	88
Money	88
Paying	89
Luggage	90
Repairs	91
Laundry	92
Complaints	92
Problems	93
Emergencies	95
Health	99
Pharmacy	99
Doctor	100
Dentist	102
Different types of travellers	104
Disabled travellers	104
With kids	106

Reference	107
Measurements and quantities	107
Numbers	109
Days and months	111
Time	114
Time phrases	116
Eating out	117
Eating places	117
In a bar/café	118
In a restaurant	121
Reading the menu	122
Vegetarian	127
Wines and spirits	129
Menu reader	132
Phonetic menu reader	147
Grammar	163
Public holidays	173
Dictionary	
English – Greek	174
Greek – English	216

Pronouncing Greek

Greek alphabet

Greek is spelt exactly as it sounds. The only difficulty may occur with letters which have the same sound, e.g. υ, η, ι or ει, οι and with double consonants. The names of the 24 letters of the Greek alphabet are given below:

			sound
α, Α	άλφα	alfa	ah
β, Β	βήτα	veeta	v
γ, Γ	γάμα	ghama	gh
δ, Δ	δέλτα	dhelta	dh
ε, Ε	έψιλον	epseelon	eh
ζ, Ζ	ζήτα	zeeta	z
η, Η	ήτα	eeta	ee
θ, Θ	θήτα	theeta	th
ι, Ι	γιώτα	yota	ee
κ, Κ	κάπα	kapa	k
λ, Λ	λάμδα	lamdha	l
μ, Μ	μι	mee	m
ν, Ν	νι	nee	n
ξ, Ξ	ξι	ksee	ks
ο, Ο	όμικρον	omeekron	oh
π, Π	πι	pee	p

				sound
ρ, Ρ	ρο	ro		r
σ, ς, Σ	σίγμα	seeghma		s
τ, Τ	ταυ	taf		t
υ, Υ	ύψιλον	eepseelon		ee
φ, Φ	φι	fee		f
χ, Χ	χι	khee		kh
ψ, Ψ	ψι	psee		ps
ω, Ω	ωμέγα	omegha		oh

In the pronunciation system used here, Greek sounds
are represented by spellings of the nearest possible
sounds in English. When you read the pronunciation
guide, pronounce the letters as if reading English.
The **bold** shows where the stress falls in the word
(in the Greek script it is marked with an accent).

	remarks	example	pronunciation
gh	like **r** at back of throat	γάλα	gh**a**la
	where γ is followed by ι or ε, it's	για	(ya)
dh	like **th** in this	δάχτυλο	dh**a**khteelo
th	like **th** in thin	θέατρο	th**e**atro
ks	like **x** in fox	ξένος	ks**e**nos
r	slightly trilled **r**	ρόδα	r**o**dha
kh	like **ch** in loch	χάνω	kh**a**no
	or like a rough **h**	χέρι	kh**e**ree

8

Here are a few tricky letter combinations:

αι	e	met	γυναίκα	yeen**e**ka
αυ	af	café	αυτό	aft**o**
	av	or **have**	αύριο	**a**vreeo
ει	ee	m**ee**t	είκοσι	**ee**kosee
ευ	ef	**eff**ect	Δευτέρα	dheft**e**ra
	ev	or **every**	Ευρώπη	evro**pee**
γγ	ng	ha**ng**	Αγγλία	angl**ee**a
γκ	g	**g**et	γκάζι	**g**azee
	ng	ha**ng**	άγκυρα	**a**ngeera
ντ	nd	ha**nd**	αντίο	and**ee**o
	d	**d**og	ντομάτα	dom**a**ta
μπ	b	**b**ag	μπλούζα	bl**oo**za
οι	ee	m**ee**t	πλοίο	pl**ee**o
ου	oo	m**oo**n	ούζο	**oo**zo

The letters η, ι, υ, οι, and ει have the same sound **ee** and αι and ε have the same sound **e** (as in m<u>e</u>t). You should also note that the Greek question mark is a semi-colon, i.e. ;.

Top ten tips

●●

1   Don't wear beachwear anywhere but at the
    beach.

2   'Yes' is signified by a slight downward nod of the
    head; 'no' is a slight upward nod of the head.

3   Nodding your head to indicate 'yes' is not polite;
    say 'yes' instead.

4   One of the rudest gestures is to thrust the palm
    of your hand in front of someone's face.

5   It's illegal to play electronic games in cybercafés
    and in public.

6   Be prepared to be asked about your age, your
    marital status, etc. Personal questions are
    commonplace and are not considered rude.

7   Easter is celebrated more than Christmas.

8   Codeine is available on prescription only, so
    medicines containing codeine should not be
    brought into Greece.

9   If your passport is stolen, call the tourist police first and they can often act as translators.

10 Names are attached to particular days of the year. For example, if you are called Elena you will celebrate your name day on May 21st. Name day celebrations are as important as birthdays!

Talking to people

Hello/goodbye, yes/no

There are two forms of address in Greek, formal and informal. Greek people use the formal until they are on a first name basis.

Yes	**Ναι** ne
No	**Όχι** **o**khee
OK	**Εντάξει** end**a**ksee
Please	**Παρακαλώ** parakal**o**
Don't mention it	**Παρακαλώ** parakal**o**
Excuse me!/sorry!	**Συγνώμη!** seeghn**o**mee!
Thank you	**Ευχαριστώ** efkhareest**o**

Thanks very much	**Ευχαριστώ πολύ**	
	efkhareest**o** pol**ee**	
Sir/Mr	**Κύριε**	
	k**ee**ree-e	
Madam/Mrs/Ms	**Κυρία**	
	keer**ee**a	
Miss	**Δεσποινίς**	
	dhespeen**ee**s	
Hello and	**Γειά σας** (formal)	
goodbye	y**a** sas	
	Γειά σου (informal)	
	y**a** soo	
Hello	**Χαίρετε**	
	kh**e**rete	
Goodbye	**Αντίο**	
	and**ee**o	
Good morning	**Καλημέρα**	
	kaleem**e**ra	
Good evening	**Καλησπέρα**	
	kaleesp**e**ra	
Good night	**Καληνύχτα**	
	kaleen**ee**khta	
How are you?	**Τι κάνετε;** (formal)	
	tee k**a**nete?	
	Τι κάνεις; (informal)	
	tee k**a**nees?	
Very well	**Πολύ καλά**	
	pol**ee** kal**a**	

14

And you?	**Εσείς;**
	es**ee**s?
I don't understand	**Δεν καταλαβαίνω**
	dhen katalav**e**no
Do you understand?	**Καταλαβαίνετε;**
	katalav**e**nete?
Do you speak English?	**Μιλάτε αγγλικά;**
	meel**a**te angleek**a**?
I speak very little Greek	**Μιλάω πολύ λίγα ελληνικά**
	meel**a**o pol**ee** l**ee**gha eleeneek**a**

Key phrases

• •

The easiest way to ask for something is by naming
what you want and adding the word for please,
parakalo.

the (masculine)	**o**
	o
(feminine)	**η**
	ee
(neuter)	**το**
	to
the coffee	**ο καφές**
	o kaf**es**

15

the beer	**η μπύρα**
	ee b**ee**ra
the glass	**το ποτήρι**
	to pot**ee**ree
a/one coffee	**ένας καφές**
	enas kaf**e**s
a/one beer	**μία μπύρα**
	m**ee**a b**ee**ra
a/one glass	**ένα ποτήρι**
	ena pot**ee**ree
a coffee, please	**έναν καφέ, παρακαλώ**
	enan kaf**e** parakal**o**
a beer, please	**μία μπύρα, παρακαλώ**
	m**ee**a b**ee**ra parakal**o**
a glass of wine, please	**ένα ποτήρι κρασί, παρακαλώ**
	ena pot**ee**ree kras**ee** parakal**o**
my passport	**το διαβατήριό μου**
	to dheeavat**ee**ree**o** moo
my room	**το δωμάτιό μου**
	to dhom**a**tee**o** moo
I'd like...	**Θα ήθελα...**
	tha **ee**thela...
I'd like an ice cream	**Θα ήθελα ένα παγωτό**
	tha **ee**thela **e**na paghot**o**
We'd like...	**Θα θέλαμε...**
	tha th**e**lame...
We'd like two rooms	**Θα θέλαμε δύο δωμάτια**
	tha th**e**lame dh**ee**o dhom**a**teea

16

We'd like to go to Athens	Θα θέλαμε να πάμε στην Αθήνα
	tha th**e**lame na p**a**me steen ath**ee**na
Do you have...?	Έχετε...;
	ekhete...?
Do you have bread?	Έχετε ψωμί;
	ekhete psom**ee**?
Do you have milk?	Έχετε γάλα;
	ekhete gh**a**la?
How much is it?	Πόσο κάνει;
	p**o**so k**a**nee?
How much does ... cost?	Πόσο κοστίζει ο/η/το...;
	p**o**so kost**ee**zee o/ee/to...?
How much is the wine?	Πόσο κάνει το κρασί;
	p**o**so k**a**nee to kras**ee**?
How much does the ticket cost?	Πόσο κοστίζει το εισιτήριο;
	p**o**so kost**ee**zee to eeseet**ee**reeo?
large	μεγάλο
	megh**a**lo
small	μικρό
	meekr**o**
with	με
	me
without	χωρίς
	khor**ee**s
Where is...?	Πού είναι...;
	poo **ee**ne...?

Where is the toilet?	**Πού είναι η τουαλέτα;**
	poo **ee**ne ee tooal**e**ta?
Where is the nearest bank?	**Πού είναι η κοντινότερη τράπεζα;**
	poo **ee**ne ee kondeen**o**teree tr**a**peza?
When does it open?	**Πότε ανοίγει;**
	p**o**te an**ee**yee?
When does it close?	**Πότε κλείνει;**
	pote kl**ee**nee?
today	**σήμερα**
	s**ee**mera
tonight	**απόψε**
	ap**o**pse
tomorrow	**αύριο**
	avreeo
yesterday	**χθες**
	khthes
Can I...?	**Μπορώ να...;**
	bor**o** na...?
Can I pay?	**Μπορώ να πληρώσω;**
	bor**o** na pleer**o**so?

Signs and notices

ΑΝΟΙΚΤΟ	open
ΚΛΕΙΣΤΟ	closed
ΣΕΛΦ ΣΕΡΒΙΣ	self-service
ΕΙΣΟΔΟΣ	entrance
ΕΞΟΔΟΣ	exit
ΤΑΜΕΙΟ	cash desk
ΩΘΗΣΑΤΕ	push
ΣΥΡΑΤΕ	pull
ΤΟΥΑΛΕΤΕΣ	toilets
ΚΕΝΤΡΟ	centre
ΑΝΔΡΩΝ	gents
ΓΥΝΑΙΚΩΝ	ladies
ΔΕΝ ΛΕΙΤΟΥΡΓΕΙ	out of order
ΚΑΤΕΙΛΗΜΜΕΝΟ	engaged
ΠΛΗΡΟΦΟΡΙΕΣ	information
ΕΝΟΙΚΙΑΖΕΤΑΙ	for hire/to rent
ΠΩΛΕΙΤΑΙ	for sale
ΕΚΠΤΩΣΕΙΣ	sales
ΔΩΜΑΤΙΑ	rooms
ΜΟΥΣΕΙΟ	museum
ΙΔΙΩΤΙΚΟΣ ΧΩΡΟΣ	private
ΗΜΕΡΟΜΗΝΙΑ	date
ΜΗΝ ΑΓΓΙΖΕΤΕ	do not touch
ΑΠΑΓΟΡΕΥΕΤΑΙ ΤΟ ΜΠΑΝΙΟ	no bathing

ΑΠΑΓΟΡΕΥΕΤΑΙ Η ΕΙΣΟΔΟΣ	no entry
ΚΑΠΝΙΖΟΝΤΕΣ	smoking
ΑΠΑΓΟΡΕΥΕΤΑΙ ΤΟ ΚΑΠΝΙΣΜΑ	no smoking
ΑΠΑΓΟΡΕΥΕΤΑΙ Η ΣΤΑΘΜΕΥΣΗ	no parking
ΑΠΑΓΟΡΕΥΕΤΑΙ Η ΚΑΤΑΣΚΗΝΩΣΗ	no camping
ΑΠΑΓΟΡΕΥΕΤΑΙ Η ΕΙΣΟΔΟΣ	no entry
ΙΣΟΓΕΙΟ	ground floor
ΕΙΣΙΤΗΡΙΑ	tickets
ΕΟΤ	Greek Tourist Office
ΦΥΛΑΞΗ ΑΠΟΣΚΕΥΩΝ	left luggage

Polite expressions

●●●●●●●●●●●●●●●●●●●●●●●●●●●●●●●●●●●●

Don't worry about making mistakes. Greek people appreciate any attempt at speaking their language. You will often be greeted with **kalos eerthate**, meaning welcome.

The meal was delicious	**Το φαγητό ήταν νοστιμότατο**
	to fa-yeet**o ee**tan nosteem**o**tato
Thank you very much	**Σας ευχαριστώ πολύ**
	sas efkhareest**o** pol**ee**
This is a gift for you	**Είναι ένα δώρο για σας**
	eene **e**na dh**o**ro ya sas
Pleased to meet you	**Χάρηκα για τη γνωριμία**
	kh**a**reeka ya tee ghnoreem**ee**a
This is my husband	**Από 'δω ο σύζυγός μου**
	ap**o** dho o s**ee**zeegh**o**s moo
This is my wife	**Από 'δω η σύζυγός μου**
	ap**o** dho ee s**ee**zeegh**o**s moo

Celebrations

I wish you a...	**Σας εύχομαι...**
	sas **e**fkhome...
I wish you a... (informal)	**Σου εύχομαι...**
	soo **e**fkhome...
Merry Christmas!	**Καλά Χριστούγεννα**
	kal**a** khreest**oo**yena
Happy New Year!	**Καλή χρονιά**
	kal**ee** khrony**a**
Happy birthday!	**Χρόνια πολλά**
	khr**o**nya pol**a**
Cheers!	**γεια μας!**
	ya mas!

Making friends

●●

In this section we have used the informal form for
the questions.

FACE TO FACE

A Πώς σε λένε;
pos se lene?
What's your name?

B Με λένε...
me lene...
My name is...

A Από πού είσαι;
apo poo eese?
Where are you from?

B Είμαι Άγγλος από το Λονδίνο
eeme anglos apo to londhino
I am English, from London

A Χάρηκα!
kharika!
Pleased to meet you!

How old are you?	**Πόσων χρονών είσαι;**
	poson khronon eese?
I'm ... years old	**Είμαι ... χρονών**
	eeme ... khronon

Are you from Greece?	**Είσαι από την Ελλάδα;**
	eese apo teen el**a**dha?
I'm from England/ Scotland	**Είμαι από την Αγγλία/ Σκωτία**
	eeme apo teen angl**ee**a/skot**ee**a
Where do you live?	**Πού μένεις;**
	p**oo** m**e**nees?
Where do you live? (plural)	**Πού μένετε;**
	p**oo** m**e**nete
I live in London	**Ζω στο Λονδίνο**
	zo sto londh**ee**no
We live in Glasgow	**Ζούμε στη Γλασκώβη**
	z**oo**me stee ghlask**o**vee
I work	**Εργάζομαι**
	ergh**a**zome
I'm retired	**Είμαι συνταξιούχος**
	eeme seendaksee**oo**khos
I'm...	**Είμαι...**
	eeme...
single	**ελεύθερος(-η)**
	el**e**fther-os(-ee)
married	**παντρεμένος(-η)**
	pandrem**e**n-os(-ee)
I have...	**Έχω...**
	ekho...
a boyfriend	**ένα φίλο**
	ena f**ee**lo
a girlfriend	**μία φίλη**
	m**ee**a f**ee**lee

24

I have ... children	Έχω ... παιδιά
	ekho ... pedhy**a**
I have no children	Δεν έχω παιδιά
	dhen **e**kho pedhy**a**
I'm here...	Βρίσκομαι εδώ...
	vr**ee**skome edh**o**...
on holiday	για διακοπές
	ya dheeakop**es**
for work	για δουλειά
	ya dhoolya

Work

....

What work do you do?	Τι δουλειά κάνετε;
	tee dhoolya k**a**nete?
Do you enjoy it?	Σας αρέσει;
	sas ar**e**see?
I'm...	Είμαι...
	eeme...
a doctor	γιατρός
	yatr**o**s
a teacher (male/female)	δάσκαλος/δασκάλα
	dh**a**skalos/dhask**a**la
I'm self-employed	Έχω δουλειά δική μου
	eho dhoolya dheek**ee** moo

Weather

•••••••••••••••••••••••••••••••••••••••

It's sunny	**Έχει ήλιο**
	ekhee **ee**lyo
It's very hot	**Κάνει πολύ ζέστη**
	k**a**nee pol**ee** z**e**stee
It's windy	**Έχει αέρα**
	ekhee a**e**ra
What awful weather!	**Τι απαίσιος καιρός!**
	tee ap**e**seeos ker**o**s!
What will the weather be like tomorrow?	**Τι καιρό θα κάνει αύριο;**
	tee ker**o** tha k**a**nee **a**vreeo?
What is the temperature?	**Τι θερμοκρασία έχει;**
	tee thermokras**ee**a **e**khee?

Getting around

Asking the way

απέναντι apenantee	opposite
δίπλα στο/στην dheepla sto/steen	next to
κοντά στο/στην konda sto/steen	near to
φανάρια fanarya	traffic lights
στη γωνία stee ghoneea	at the corner
στην πλατεία steen plateea	in the square

I'm looking for...	ψάχνω για... psakhno ya...
Can I walk there?	Μπορώ να πάω με τα πόδια; boro na pao me ta podhya?
We're lost	Έχουμε χαθεί ekhoome khathee
Is this the way to...?	Πάω καλά για...; pao kala ya...?

27

FACE TO FACE

A Με συγχωρείτε! Πώς θα πάω στο σταθμό;

me seenkhor**ee**te! p**o**s tha p**a**o sto stathm**o**?

Excuse me, how do I get to the station?

B Όλο ευθεία και μετά την εκκλησία στρίψτε
αριστερά/δεξιά!

olo efth**ee**a ke met**a** teen eklees**ee**a str**i**pste
areester**a**/dheks**ee**a!

Keep straight on, after the church turn left/right!

A Είναι μακρυά;

eene makree**a**?

Is it far?

B Όχι, περίπου 400 μ/πέντε λεπτά

okhi, per**ee**pou 400 m./p**e**nte lept**a**

No, 4 metres/five minutes

A Ευχαριστώ!

efkharist**o**!

Thank you!

B Παρακαλώ

parakal**o**

You're welcome

28

Is it far?	Είναι μακριά;
	eene makree**a**?
How do I get onto the motorway?	Πώς θα βγω στην εθνική οδό;
	p**o**s tha vgho steen ethneek**ee** odh**o**?
Can you show me where it is on the map?	Μπορείτε να μου το δείξετε πάνω στο χάρτη;
	bor**ee**te na moo to dh**ee**ksete p**a**no sto kh**a**rtee?

YOU MAY HEAR...

Στρίψτε δεξιά/αριστερά str**ee**pste dheksee**a**/areester**a**	Turn right/left
Προχωρήστε ευθεία μέχρι να φτάσετε... prokhor**ee**ste efth**ee**a m**e**khree na ft**a**sete...	Keep straight on until you get...
στη διασταύρωση stee dheeast**a**vrosee	to the junction

> **Maps and guides** (p 69)

29

Bus and coach

....

Bus is the major form of overland transport in
Greece and Cyprus and there is a good network of
local and long-distance routes. On some routes you
must buy a ticket before you depart.

FACE TO FACE

A Συγνώμη, ποιό λεωφορείο πάει στο
κέντρο;
seeghn**o**mee, py**o** lefor**ee**o p**a**ee sto k**e**ntro?
Excuse me, which bus goes to the centre?

B Το νούμερο 15
to n**oo**mero 15
Number 15

A Πού είναι η στάση;
poo **ee**ne ee st**a**see?
Where is the bus stop?

B Εκεί δεξιά
ek**ee** dhekse**a** .
There, on the right

A Πού μπορώ να αγοράσω εισιτήρια;
poo bor**o** na aghor**a**so eeseet**ee**reea?
Where can I buy tickets?

B Στο περίπτερο
sto per**ee**ptero
At the kiosk

Is there a bus to...?	**Υπάρχει λεωφορείο για...;** eep**a**rkhee leefor**ee**o ya...?
Where do I catch the bus to...?	**Από πού θα πάρω το λεωφορείο για...;** ap**o** poo tha p**a**ro to leefor**ee**o ya...?
We're going to...	**Πηγαίνουμε στο...** peey**e**noome sto...
How much is it...?	**Πόσο κάνει...;** p**o**so k**a**nee...?
to the beach	**για τη θάλασσα** ya tee th**a**lasa
to the airport	**για το αεροδρόμιο** ya to aerodhr**o**meeo
How often are the buses to...?	**Κάθε πότε έχει λεωφορείο για...;** k**a**the p**o**te **e**khee leefor**ee**o ya...?
When is	**Πότε είναι** p**o**te **ee**ne
the first	**το πρώτο** to pr**o**to
the last	**το τελευταίο** to telef**te**o
bus	**λεωφορείο** leefor**ee**o
to...?	**για...;** ya ...?

| Please can you tell me when to get off? | Παρακαλώ, μπορείτε να μου πείτε πότε να κατέβω;
parakalo boreete na moo peete pote na katevo? |
| This is my stop | Αυτή είναι η στάση μου
aftee eene ee stasee moo |

YOU MAY HEAR...

| Το λεωφορείο αυτό δε σταματά στο...
to leoforeeo afto dhe stamata sto... | This bus doesn't stop in... |
| Πρέπει να πάρετε το...
prepee na parete to... | You have to catch the... |

Metro

The new metro system in Athens opens at 5.30 am and closes at midnight. A ticket is valid for one single journey of any length. You can also get a 24-hour ticket. There are armed police on patrol at stations. It is forbidden to eat or drink in the stations and on the metro.

| Where is the metro station? | Πού είναι ο σταθμός του μετρό;
poo eene o stathmos too metro? |

(for old electric line)	**του ηλεκτρικού;**
	too eelektreek**oo**?
A ticket	**Ένα εισιτήριο**
	ena eeseet**ee**reeo
A 24-hour ticket	**Ένα ημερήσιο εισιτήριο**
	ena eemer**ee**seeo eeseet**ee**reeo
4 tickets, please	**Τέσσερα εισιτήρια**
	παρακαλώ
	t**e**sera eeseet**ee**reea parakal**o**
Do you have an underground map?	**Έχετε ένα χάρτη με τις γραμμές του μετρό;**
	ekhete **e**na kh**a**rtee me tees ghramm**e**s too metr**o**?
I want to go to...	**Θέλω να πάω στο/στη...**
	th**e**lo na p**a**o sto/stee...
Do I have to change?	**Πρέπει να αλλάξω τρένο;**
	pr**e**pee na al**a**kso tr**e**no?
Where?	**Πού;**
	poo?
Which line do I take?	**Ποια γραμμή πρέπει να πάρω;**
	pya ghramm**ee** pr**e**pee na p**a**ro?

Metro

33

Train

Train services in Greece are limited and slow by comparison with other western European railways. There is only one main line, operated by Greek Railways ΟΣΕ, running from Athens north to Thessaloniki and onwards to Bulgaria, Turkey and the former Yugoslavia. The Peloponnese is served by a narrow-gauge line from Athens. There are no trains on Cyprus.

FACE TO FACE

A Πότε είναι το τρένο για...;
pote **ee**ne to tr**e**no ya...?
When is the train to...?

B Στις πέντε και δέκα
stees p**e**nte ke dh**e**ka
At ten past five

A Θα ήθελα δύο εισιτήρια παρακαλώ
tha **ee**thela dh**ee**o eeseet**ee**reea parakal**o**
I'd like two tickets, please

B απλό εισιτήριο ή με επιστροφή;
apl**o** eeseet**ee**reeo **ee** me epeestrof**ee**?
Single or return?

Where is the train station?	Πού είναι ο σταθμός τρένου; poo **ee**ne o stathm**os** tr**e**noo?

To the station, please	**Στο σταθμό παρακαλώ**
	sto stathm**o** parakal**o**
A single to...	**Ένα απλό εισιτήριο για…**
	ena apl**o** eeseet**ee**reeo ya...
Two singles to...	**Δύο απλά εισιτήρια για…**
	dh**ee**o apl**a** eeseet**ee**reea ya...
A return to...	**Ένα εισιτήριο με επιστροφή για…**
	ena eeseet**ee**reeo me epeestrof**ee** ya...
Two return tickets to...	**Δύο εισιτήρια με επιστροφή για…**
	dh**ee**o eeseet**ee**reea me epeestrof**ee** ya...
Economy class	**Τουριστική θέση**
	tooreesteek**ee** th**e**see
Smoking	**Καπνίζοντες**
	kapn**ee**zontes
Non smoking	**Μη καπνίζοντες**
	mee kapn**ee**zontes
I want to book a seat to Thessaloniki	**Θέλω να κλείσω ένα εισιτήριο για τη Θεσσαλονίκη**
	th**e**lo na kl**ee**so **e**na eeseet**ee**reeo ya tee thesalon**ee**kee
When does it arrive in...?	**Πότε φτάνει στο…;**
	p**o**te ft**a**nee sto...?
Do I have to change?	**Πρέπει να αλλάξω;**
	pr**e**pee na al**a**kso?

Where?	**Πού;**
	poo?
Which platform does it leave from?	**Από ποια πλατφόρμα φεύγει;**
	ap**o** pya platf**o**rma f**e**vyee?
Is this the train for...?	**Αυτό είναι το τρένο για...;**
	aft**o ee**ne to tr**e**no ya...?
When will it leave?	**Πότε θα φύγει;**
	p**o**te tha f**ee**yee?
Why is the train delayed?	**Γιατί έχει καθυστέρηση το τρένο;**
	yat**ee e**khee katheest**e**reesee to tr**e**no?
Does the train stop at...?	**Σταματάει το τρένο στο...;**
	stamat**a**ee to tr**e**no sto...?
Please let me know when we get to...	**Μου λέτε, σας παρακαλώ, πότε φτάνουμε στο...**
	moo l**e**te, sas parakal**o**, p**o**te ft**a**noome sto...
Is this free? (seat)	**Είναι ελεύθερη;**
	eene el**e**ftheree?
Excuse me	**Με συγχωρείτε**
	me seenkhor**ee**te

> **Luggage** (p 90)

Taxi

....

If you plan to take a taxi from the airport, check with
the information desk how much the fare should be.

I need a taxi	**Χρειάζομαι ταξί**
	khree**a**zome taks**ee**
Where can I get a taxi?	**Πού μπορώ να πάρω ένα ταξί;**
	poo bor**o** na p**a**ro **e**na taks**ee**?
How much is a taxi...?	**Πόσο κάνει το ταξί...;**
	p**o**so k**a**nee to taks**ee**...?
to the station	**για το σταθμό**
	ya to stathm**o**
to the airport	**για το αεροδρόμιο**
	ya to aerodhr**o**meeo
to the centre	**για το κέντρο**
	ya to k**e**ntro
Please take me (us) to...	**Παρακαλώ πηγαίνετέ με (μας) στο...**
	parakal**o** peey**e**net**e** me (mas) sto...
Why are you charging me so much?	**Γιατί με χρεώνετε τόσο πολύ;**
	yat**ee** me khre**o**nete t**o**so pol**ee**?
Keep the change	**Κρατήστε τα ρέστα**
	krat**ee**ste ta r**e**sta

Sorry, I don't have change	Συγνώμη, δεν έχω ψιλά
	seeghnomee, dhen ekho pseela
I have to catch...	Πρέπει να προλάβω...
	prepee na prolavo...
the ... o'clock flight to...	την πτήση των ... για το...
	teen pteesee ton ... ya to...

Boat and ferry

In Greece, with its many islands, ferries are an important means of transport. The centre of the ferry network is the port of Piraeus. Hydrofoils – ιπτάμενο δελφίνι (eeptameno dhelfeenee) 'flying dolphins' – operate between Piraeus and the nearer islands.

When is the next boat to...?	Πότε φεύγει το επόμενο πλοίο για...;
	pote fevyee to epomeno pleeo ya...?
Have you a timetable?	Έχετε ωρολόγιο πρόγραμμα;
	ekhete oroloyeeo proghrama?
Is there a boat to...?	Υπάρχει πλοίο για...;
	eeparkhee pleeo ya...?
How much is a ticket...?	Πόσο κάνει ένα εισιτήριο...;
	poso kanee ena eeseeteereeo...?

38

single	**απλό**
	apl**o**
return	**με επιστροφή**
	me epeestrof**ee**
How long is the journey?	**Πόσο διαρκεί το ταξίδι;**
	p**o**so dheeark**ee** to taks**ee**dhee?
What time do we get to...?	**Τι ώρα φτάνουμε στο...;**
	tee **o**ra ft**a**noome sto...?
Where does the boat leave from?	**Από πού φεύγει το πλοίο;**
	ap**o** poo f**e**vyee to pl**ee**o?
When is...?	**Πότε είναι...;**
	p**o**te **ee**ne...?
the first...	**το πρώτο...**
	to pr**o**to...
the last...	**το τελευταίο...**
	to teleft**e**o...
hydrofoil	**ιπτάμενο δελφίνι**
	eept**a**meno dhelf**ee**nee
boat	**πλοίο**
	pl**ee**o
ferry	**φεριμπότ**
	fereeb**o**t

Air travel

Most signs are in Greek and English and you may go through the airport without having to speak any Greek. If you are arriving at Athens on a non-Greek carrier and have a domestic flight to catch, allow plenty of time to get across the airport. Greece is highly security-conscious and it is against the law to take photographs of airports.

ΑΦΙΞΕΙΣ afeeksees	arrivals
ΕΙΣΟΔΟΣ eesodhos	entrance
ΕΞΟΔΟΣ eksodhos	exit
ΑΝΑΧΩΡΗΣΕΙΣ anakhoreesees	departures
ΠΤΗΣΗ pteesee	flight

To the airport, please	**Στο αεροδρόμιο, παρακαλώ** sto aerodhromeeo, parakalo
How do I get to the airport?	**Πώς μπορώ να πάω στο αεροδρόμιο;** pos boro na pao sto aerodhromeeo
Is there a bus to the city centre?	**Υπάρχει λεωφορείο για το κέντρο της πόλης;** eeparkhee leoforeeo ya to kendro tees polees?

Where do I check in for...(airline)?	Πού γίνεται ο έλεγχος αποσκευών για...;
	poo y**ee**nete o **e**lenhos aposkev**o**n ya...?
Which gate is it for the flight to...?	Ποια είναι η έξοδος της πτήσης για...;
	pya **ee**ne ee **e**ksodhos tees pt**ee**sees ya...?

> **Luggage** (p 90) > **Taxi** (p 37)

Customs control

●●

Getting around

You will not be allowed to enter Greece or Cyprus if
your passport has a stamp from the Turkish Republic
of Northern Cyprus. You will need an export permit
if you plan to take home any antiquities, including
old icons, even if they appear to have little or no
archaeological or commercial value. Both the Greek
and Cypriot authorities are very sensitive about the
illegal export of antiquities, so should you be caught
do not expect clemency. With the single European
market, passengers arriving from a member state of
the European Union are subject only to highly
selective spot checks and they can
go through the blue customs channel.

Do I have to pay duty on this?	**Πρέπει να πληρώσω φόρο γι' αυτό;** prepee na pleeroso foro yafto?
It is for my own personal use	**Είναι για προσωπική μου χρήση** eene ya prosopeekee moo khreesee
We are on our way to...	**Πηγαίνουμε για…** peegenoome ya…

Driving

Car hire

το δίπλωμα οδήγησης	driving licence
to dh**ee**ploma odh**ee**yeesees	
η οπίσθεν ee **o**peesthen	reverse gear

I want to hire a car	**Θέλω να νοικιάσω ένα αυτοκίνητο**
	th**e**lo na neeky**a**so **e**na aftok**ee**neeto
for ... days	**για ... μέρες**
	ya ... m**e**res
How much is it...?	**Πόσο κάνει...;**
	p**o**so k**a**nee...?
per day	**τη μέρα**
	tee m**e**ra
per week	**τη βδομάδα**
	tee vdhom**a**dha
How much is the deposit?	**Πόση είναι η προκαταβολή;**
	p**o**see **ee**ne ee prokatavol**ee**?

Is there a charge per kilometre?	Γίνεται χρέωση ανά χιλιόμετρο;
	yeenete khreosee ana kheelyometro?
What is included in the insurance?	Τι περιλαμβάνεται στην ασφάλεια;
	tee pereelamvanete steen asfaleea?
Do I have to return the car here?	Πρέπει να γυρίσω το αυτοκίνητο εδώ;
	prepee na yeereeso to aftokeeneeto edho?
What time?	Τι ώρα;
	tee ora?
I'd like to leave it in...	Θα ήθελα να το αφήσω στο…
	tha eethela na to afeeso sto…
What do I do if I break down?	Τι θα κάνω αν μείνω από βλάβη;
	tee tha kano an meeno apo vlavee?

YOU MAY HEAR...

Μπορείτε να γυρίσετε το αυτοκίνητο με άδειο ρεζερβουάρ	You can return the car with an empty tank
boreete na yeereesete to aftokeeneeto me adheeo rezervooar	

44

Motorbike hire

Hiring a motorbike is a popular and economical form of transport in both Greece and Cyprus. Motorbikes are however the cause of a great number of injuries. Regulations requiring the wearing of crash helmets are widely flouted. When hiring, check that the machine is mechanically sound and that insurance is provided.

I want to hire...	**Θέλω να νοικιάσω…** th**e**lo na neeky**a**so...
a motorcycle	**μοτοσυκλέτα** motoseekl**e**ta
a moped	**μοτοποδήλατο** motopodh**ee**lato
for a day	**για μία μέρα** ya m**ee**a m**e**ra
for the morning	**για το πρωί** ya to pro**ee**
for the afternoon	**για το απόγευμα** ya to ap**o**yevma
Is a crash helmet included in the price?	**Το κράνος περιλαμβάνεται στην τιμή;** to kr**a**nos pereelamv**a**nete steen teem**ee**?

45

Is insurance included in the price?	Η ασφάλιση περιλαμβάνεται στην τιμή;
	ee asf**a**leesee pereelamv**a**nete steen teem**ee**?
I want to pay by credit card	Θέλω να πληρώσω με πιστωτική κάρτα
	th**e**lo na pleer**o**so me peestoteek**ee** k**a**rta
What is your phone number?	Ποιος είναι ο αριθμός του τηλεφώνου σας;
	pyos **ee**ne o areethm**o**s too teelef**o**noo sas?

Driving

Try to avoid driving in the major cities, particularly Athens. Traffic congestion can be appalling and parking in city centres almost impossible. Drive on the right in Greece but on the left in Cyprus.

Can I park here?	**Μπορώ να παρκάρω εδώ;**
	bor**o** na park**a**ro edh**o**?
How long for?	**Για πόση ώρα;**
	ya p**o**see **o**ra?
Where can I park?	**Πού μπορώ να παρκάρω;**
	poo bor**o** na park**a**ro?
Do I need a parking ticket?	**Χρειάζομαι κάρτα στάθμευσης;**
	khree**a**zome k**a**rta st**a**thmefsees?
We're going to...	**Πηγαίνουμε στο…**
	peey**e**noome sto...
Which junction is it for...?	**Σε ποια διασταύρωση είναι…;**
	se pya dheeast**a**vrosee **ee**ne...?

Petrol

....

ΑΜΟΛΥΒΔΗ amoleevdhee	unleaded
ΠΕΤΡΕΛΑΙΟ petreleo	diesel
ΒΕΝΖΙΝΗ venzeenee	petrol

Is there a petrol station near here?
Υπάρχει βενζινάδικο εδώ κοντά;
eeparkhee venzeenadheeko edho konda?

Fill it up, please
Γεμίστε το, παρακαλώ
yemeeste to parakalo

Please check the oil/the water
Παρακαλώ ελέγξτε τα λάδια/το νερό
parakalo elenkste ta ladhya/to nero

20 euros worth of unleaded petrol
Είκοσι ευρώ αμόλυβδη βενζίνη
eekosee evro amoleevdhee venzeenee

Where is...?
Πού είναι...;
poo eene...?

the air line
η παροχή του αέρα
ee parokhee too aera

the water
το νερό
to nero

Please check the tyres	**Παρακαλώ ελέγξτε τα λάστιχα**
	parakalo elenkste ta lasteekha
Can I pay with this credit card?	**Μπορώ να πληρώσω με αυτή την κάρτα;**
	boro na pleeroso me aftee tee karta?

Breakdown

Can you help me?	**Μπορείτε να με βοηθήσετε;**
	boreete na me voeetheesete?
My car has broken down	**Το αυτοκίνητό μου χάλασε**
	to aftokeeneeto moo khalase
Is there a garage near here?	**Υπάρχει συνεργείο εδώ κοντά;**
	eeparkhee seeneryeeo edho konda?
The car won't start	**Το αυτοκίνητο δεν ξεκινά**
	to aftokeeneeto dhen ksekeena
Can you give me a push?	**Μπορείτε να σπρώξετε;**
	boreete na sproksete?
I've run out of petrol	**Έμεινα από βενζίνη**
	emeena apo venzeenee

Can you tow me to the nearest garage?	Μπορείτε να με τραβήξετε μέχρι το κοντινότερο συνεργείο;
	boreete na me traveeksete mekhree to kondeenotero seeneryeeo?

Car parts

The ... doesn't work	ο/η/το ... δε λειτουργεί
	o/ee/to ... dhe leetooryee
The ... don't work	οι/τα ... δε λειτουργούν
	ee/ta ... dhe leetoorghoon

accelerator	το γκάζι	gazee
battery	η μπαταρία	batareea
brakes	τα φρένα	frena
choke	το τσοκ	tsok
clutch	ο συμπλέκτης	seemblektees
engine	η μηχανή	meekhanee
exhaust pipe	η εξάτμιση	eksatmeesee
fuse	η ασφάλεια	asfaleea
gears	οι ταχύτητες	takheeteetes
handbrake	το χειρόφρενο	kheerofreno
headlights	τα φώτα	ta fota
ignition	η ανάφλεξη	anafleksee
indicator	το φλας	flas

radiator	το ψυγείο	pseey**ee**o
rear lights	τα πίσω φώτα	p**ee**so f**o**ta
seat belt	η ζώνη ασφαλείας	z**o**nee asfal**ee**as
spare wheel	η ρεζέρβα	rez**e**rva
spark plug	το μπουζί	booz**ee**
steering wheel	το τιμόνι	teem**o**nee
tyre	το λάστιχο	l**a**steekho
wheel	η ρόδα	r**o**dha
windscreen	το παρμπρίζ	parbr**ee**z
wiper	ο υαλοκαθ- αριστήρας	eealokathar**ee**- st**ee**ras

Road signs

camping

customs control

restricted parking
zone

end to restricted
parking zone

directional sign

north

west

east

south

no parking in
odd-numbered
months

no parking in
even-numbered
months

motorway toll

parking for
card holders

Speed limits in Greece
are in kilometres

parking for taxis

53

Staying somewhere

Hotel (booking)

●●

It is best to book accommodation in advance, particularly in the more popular resorts in high season. If you do get stuck for a place to stay, a branch of the Greek Tourist Organisation (or Cyprus Tourism Organisation in Cyprus) may be able to help.

FACE TO FACE

A Θα ήθελα ένα δίκλινο/μονόκλινο δωμάτιο
tha **ee**thela **e**na dh**ee**kleeno/mon**o**kleeno dhom**a**teeo
I'd like a double/single room

B Για πόσες νύχτες;
ya p**o**ses n**ee**khtes?
For how many nights?

A Για μια νύχτα/... νύχτες
ya mya n**ee**khta/... n**ee**khtes
for one night/... nights

ΞΕΝΟΔΟΧΕΙΟ ksenodhokheeo	hotel
ΔΩΜΑΤΙΑ dhomateea	rooms (often in private houses)

Do you have any vacancies?	Έχετε ελεύθερα δωμάτια; ekhete eleftera dhomateea?
for tonight	για απόψε; ya apopse?
We'd like to stay ... nights	Θα θέλαμε να μείνουμε ... βράδυα tha thelame na meenoome ... vradheea
from ... till...	από ... μέχρι... apo ... mekhree...
How much is it per day/ per week?	Πόσο κοστίζει για μια μέρα/μια βδομάδα; poso kosteezee ya mya mera/ mya vdomada?
for three people	τρίκλινο treekleeno
with bath	με μπάνιο me banyo
with shower	με ντους me doos
with a double bed	με διπλό κρεβάτι me dheeplo krevatee
twin-bedded	με δύο κρεβάτια me dheeo krevatya

A room looking onto the sea	**Ένα δωμάτιο που να βλέπει στη θάλασσα**
	ena dhom**a**teeo poo na vl**e**pee stee th**a**lasa
How much is it...?	**Πόσο κοστίζει...;**
	p**o**so kost**ee**zee...?
per night	**το βράδυ**
	to vr**a**dhee
per week	**τη βδομάδα**
	tee vdhom**a**dha
for half board	**με ημιδιατροφή**
	me eemeedheeatrof**ee**
for full board	**με πλήρη διατροφή**
	me pl**ee**ree dheeatrof**ee**
Is breakfast included?	**Το πρωινό περιλαμβάνεται στην τιμή;**
	to proeen**o** pereelamv**a**nete steen teem**ee**?

YOU MAY HEAR...

Είμαστε γεμάτοι **ee**maste yem**a**tee	We're full

56

Hotel (desk)

Most hotels will provide breakfast if you ask for it.

I booked a room...	**Έκλεισα ένα δωμάτιο...**
	ekleesa **e**na dhom**a**teeo...
in the name of...	**στο όνομα...**
	sto **o**noma...
I'd like to see the room	**Θα ήθελα να δω το δωμάτιο**
	tha **ee**thela na dho to dhom**a**teeo
Where can I park?	**Πού μπορώ να παρκάρω;**
	poo bor**o** na park**a**ro?
What time is...?	**Τι ώρα σερβίρεται...;**
	tee **o**ra serv**ee**rete...?
dinner	**το δείπνο**
	to dh**ee**pno
breakfast	**το πρωινό**
	to proeen**o**
The key, please	**Το κλειδί, παρακαλώ**
	to kleedh**ee**, parakal**o**
room number...	**αριθμός δωματίου...**
	areethm**o**s dhomat**ee**oo...
Can you keep it in the safe, please?	**Μπορείτε να το φυλάξετε στο σέιφ;**
	bor**ee**te na to feel**a**ksete sto s**a**fe?

57

I'm leaving tomorrow	**Φεύγω αύριο**
	fevgho avreeo
Please prepare the bill	**Παρακαλώ ετοιμάστε το λογαριασμό**
	parakalo eteemaste to logharyasmo
Can I leave my luggage until...?	**Μπορώ να αφήσω τις βαλίτσες μου μέχρι...;**
	boro na afeeso tees valeetses moo mekhree...?

Hotel (room service)

Come in!	**Περάστε!**
	peraste!
I'd like breakfast in my room	**Θα ήθελα το πρωινό στο δωμάτιο**
	tha eethela to proeeno sto dhomateeo
Please bring me...	**Παρακαλώ φέρτε μου...**
	parakalo ferte moo...
a glass	**ένα ποτήρι**
	ena poteeree
clean towels	**καθαρές πετσέτες**
	kathares petsetes
toilet paper	**χαρτί υγείας**
	khartee eeyeeas

I'd like an early morning call tomorrow	**Θα ήθελα να με ξυπνήσετε νωρίς το πρωί** tha **ee**thela na me kseepn**ee**sete nor**ee**s to pro**ee**
at 6 o'clock	**στις έξι η ώρα** stees **e**ksee ee **o**ra
I'd like an outside line	**Θα ήθελα μία εξωτερική γραμμή** tha **ee**thela m**ee**a eksotereek**ee** ghram**ee**
This doesn't work	**Δε δουλεύει αυτό** dhe dhool**e**vee aft**o**

Camping

Although camping is not as popular as in some other European countries, Greece has a number of campsites operated by the Greek Tourist Organisation. There are six campsites on Cyprus. In both countries camping is only permitted on official sites.

Is there a restaurant on the campsite?	**Υπάρχει εστιατόριο στο κάμπινγκ;** eep**a**rkhee esteeat**o**reeo sto c**a**mping?

Do you have any vacancies?	**Έχετε ελεύθερες θέσεις;** ekhete eleftheres thesees?
Are showers.../ Is hot water.../ Is electricity...	**Οι ντουσιέρες…/το ζεστό νερό…/το ηλεκτρικό…** ee doosyeres.../to zesto nero.../ to eelektreeko...
...included in the price?	**…περιλαμβάνονται στην τιμή;** ...pereelamvanonde steen teemee?
We'd like to stay for ... nights	**Θέλουμε να μείνουμε … νύχτες** theloome na meenoome ... neekhtes
How much is it per night...?	**Πόσο κοστίζει τη νύχτα…;** poso kosteezee tee neekhta...?
for a tent	**η σκηνή** ee skeenee
per person	**το άτομο** to atomo

Self-catering

....

Who do we contact if there are problems?	**Σε ποιόν θ' απευθυνθούμε αν υπάρξουν προβλήματα;**
	se py**o**n th-apeftheenth**oo**me an eep**a**rksoon provl**ee**mata?
How does the heating work?	**Πώς λειτουργεί η θέρμανση;**
	pos leetoory**ee** ee th**e**rmansee?
Is there always hot water?	**Έχει πάντα ζεστό νερό;**
	ekhee p**a**nta zest**o** ner**o**?
Where is the nearest supermarket?	**Πού είναι το κοντινότερο supermarket;**
	poo **ee**ne to kondeen**o**tero supermarket?
Where do we leave the rubbish?	**Που πετάμε τα σκουπίδια;**
	poo pet**a**me ta skoop**ee**dhya?

> **Sightseeing and tourist office** (p 72)

Self-catering

Shopping

Shopping phrases

....

ΤΑΜΕΙΟ tam**ee**o	cash desk
ΕΔΩ ΠΛΗΡΩΝΕΤΕ edh**o** pleer**o**nete	pay here

FACE TO FACE

A **Τί θα θέλατε;**
tee tha th**e**late?
What would you like?

B **Έχετε...;**
ekhete...?
Do you have...?

A **Ναι, φυσικά. Θα θέλατε τίποτε άλλο;**
ne, feeseek**a**. Tha th**e**late t**ee**pote **a**llo?
Yes, certainly. Would you like anything else?

Where is...?	**Πού είναι...;**
	poo eene...?
Do you sell...?	**Πουλάτε...;**
	poolate...?
I'm looking for	**ψάχνω για ένα δώρο για...**
a present for...	psakhno ya ena dhoro ya...
my mother	**τη μητέρα μου**
	tee meetera moo
a child	**ένα παιδί**
	ena pedhee
Where can I	**Πού μπορώ να αγοράσω...;**
buy...?	poo boro na aghoraso...?
toys	**παιχνίδια**
	pekhneedhya
gifts	**δώρα**
	dhora
It's too expensive	**Είναι πολύ ακριβό**
	eene polee akreevo
Have you	**Έχετε τίποτε άλλο;**
anything else?	ekhete teepote alo?

Shops

baker's	ΑΡΤΟΠΟΙΕΙΟ	artopee-**ee**o
bookshop	ΒΙΒΛΙΟΠΩΛΕΙΟ	veevleeopol**ee**o
butcher's	ΚΡΕΟΠΩΛΕΙΟ	kreopol**ee**o
cake shop	ΖΑΧΑΡΟ–ΠΛΑΣΤΕΙΟ	zakharoplast**ee**o
clothes	ΕΝΔΥΜΑΤΑ	endh**ee**mata
gifts	ΔΩΡΑ	dh**o**ra
grocer's	ΠΑΝΤΟΠΩΛΕΙΟ	pantopol**ee**o
hairdresser's	ΚΟΜΜΩΤΗΡΙΟ	komoteer**ee**o
pharmacy	ΦΑΡΜΑΚΕΙΟ	farmak**ee**o
shoe shop	ΚΑΤΑΣΤΗΜΑ ΥΠΟΔΗΜΑΤΩΝ	kat**a**steema eepodheem**a**ton
shop	ΚΑΤΑΣΤΗΜΑ	kat**a**steema
stationer's	ΧΑΡΤΟΠΩΛΕΙΟ	khartopol**ee**o
supermarket	ΣΟΥΠΕΡΜΑΡΚΕΤ	s**u**permarket
toy shop	ΠΑΙΧΝΙΔΙΑ	pekhn**ee**dheea

Food (general)

biscuits	τα μπισκότα	beesk**o**ta
bread	το ψωμί	psom**ee**
butter	το βούτυρο	v**oo**teero
cheese	το τυρί	teer**ee**
chicken	το κοτόπουλο	kot**o**poolo

coffee (instant)	το Νεσκαφέ®	Nescafe
crisps	τα πατατάκια	patatakya
eggs	τα αβγά	avgha
ham	το ζαμπόν	zambon
honey	το μέλι	melee
jam	η μαρμελάδα	marmeladha
marmalade	η μαρμελάδα πορτοκάλι	marmeladha portokalee
milk	το γάλα	ghala
olive oil	το ελαιόλαδο	eleoladho
orange juice	ο χυμός πορτοκαλιού	kheemos portokalyoo
pepper	το πιπέρι	peeperee
salt	το αλάτι	alatee
sugar	η ζάχαρη	zakharee
tea	το τσάι	tsaee
vinegar	το ξύδι	kseedhee
yoghurt	το γιαούρτι	yaoortee

Food (fruit and veg)

. . . .

Fruit

apples	τα μήλα	meela
apricots	τα βερίκοκα	vereekoka
bananas	οι μπανάνες	bananes

> **Measurements and quantities** (p 107) 65

cherries	τα κεράσια	kerasya
figs	τα σύκα	seeka
grapefruit	τα γκρέιπφρουτ	grapefruit
grapes	τα σταφύλια	stafeelya
lemon	το λεμόνι	lemonee
melon	το πεπόνι	peponee
oranges	τα πορτοκάλια	portokalya
peaches	τα ροδάκινα	rodhakeena
pears	τα αχλάδια	akhladhya
strawberries	οι φράουλες	fraooles
watermelon	το καρπούζι	karpoozee

Vegetables

asparagus	τα σπαράγγια	sparanghya
carrots	τα καρότα	karota
cauliflower	το κουνουπίδι	koonoopeedhee
courgettes	τα κολοκυθάκια	kolokeethakya
cucumber	το αγγούρι	angooree
garlic	το σκόρδο	skordho
lettuce	το μαρούλι	maroolee
mushrooms	τα μανιτάρια	maneetarya
onions	τα κρεμμύδια	kremeedhya
peas	ο αρακάς	arakas
peppers	οι πιπεριές	peeperyes
potatoes	οι πατάτες	patates
spinach	το σπανάκι	spanakee
tomatoes	οι ντομάτες	domates

Clothes

The Greek for size is **νούμερο** (noomero).

women's sizes		men's suit sizes		shoe sizes			
UK	EU	UK	EU	UK	EU	UK	EU
8	36	36	46	2	35	7	41
10	38	38	48	3	36	8	42
12	40	40	50	4	37	9	43
14	42	42	52	5	38	10	44
16	44	44	54	6	39	11	45
18	46	46	56				

FACE TO FACE

A Μπορώ να το δοκιμάσω;
bor**o** na to dhokeem**a**so?
May I try this on?

B Ναι, φυσικά
ne, feeseek**a**
Yes, of course

A Έχετε μεγαλύτερο/μικρότερο νούμερο;
ekhete meghal**ee**tero/meekr**o**tero n**oo**mero?
Do you have a larger/smaller size?

B Τι νούμερο φοράτε;
tee n**oo**mero for**a**te?
What size do you take?

Where are the changing rooms?	Πού είναι τα δοκιμαστήρια;	poo eene ta dhokeemasteereea?
Do you have this...?	έχετε αυτό...;	ekhete afto...?
in my size	στο νούμερο μου	sto noomero moo
in other colours	σε άλλα χρώματα	se ala khromata
I'm just looking	Απλώς κοιτάζω	aplos keetazo
I'll take it	Θα το πάρω	tha to paro

Clothes (articles)

coat	το παλτό	palto
dress	το φόρεμα	forema
jacket	η ζακέτα	zaketa
pyjamas	οι πυτζάμες	peetzames
shirt	το πουκάμισο	pookameeso
shorts	το σορτς	sorts
skirt	η φούστα	foosta
socks	οι κάλτσες	kaltses
suit	το κοστούμι	kostoomee

> **Paying** (p 89)

swimsuit	το μαγιό	mayo
top	η μπλούζα	blooza
trousers	το παντελόνι	pandelonee
t-shirt	το μπλουζάκι	bloozakee

Maps and guides

You can buy maps and newspapers at kiosks in the big cities.

Have you...?	Έχετε...;
	ekhete...?
a map of the town	ένα χάρτη της πόλης
	ena khartee tees polees
Can you show me (name of place) on the map?	Μπορείτε να μου δείξετε ... πάνω στο χάρτη;
	boreete na moo dheeksete ... pano sto khartee?
Have you...?	Έχετε...;
	ekhete...?
a guide book	έναν οδηγό
	enan odheegho
in English	στα αγγλικά
	sta angleeka

> **Asking the way** (p 27) > **Sightseeing** (p 72)

Do you have	**Μήπως έχετε αγγλικές**
any English	**εφημερίδες/αγγλικά βιβλία;**
newspapers/	m**ee**pos **e**khete angleek**e**s
English books?	efeemer**ee**dhes/angleek**a**
	veevl**ee**a?

Post office

. . . .

Opening hours of post offices in Greece vary from place to place and according to the time of year. However, most of them close at midday, apart from those in major cities.

ΤΑΧΥΔΡΟΜΕΙΟ	post office
takheedhrom**ee**o	
ΓΡΑΜΜΑΤΟΣΗΜΑ	stamps
ghramat**o**seema	

Do you sell	**Πουλάτε γραμματόσημα;**
stamps?	pool**a**te ghramat**o**seema?
Is there a post	**Υπάρχει ταχυδρομείο εδώ**
office near	**κοντά;**
here?	eep**a**rkhee takheedhrom**ee**o edh**o**
	kond**a**?
Stamps for	**Γραμματόσημα για κάρτες**
postcards to	**για τη Μεγάλη Βρετανία**
Great Britain	ghramat**o**seema ya k**a**rtes ya tee
	megh**a**lee vretan**ee**a

70

Photos

• •

Although cassettes for camcorders and memory
cards for digital cameras can be bought in the major
towns, if you are staying in a more remote area it is
wise to take enough film/memory cards and
cassettes for your requirements.

Have you batteries...?	Έχετε μπαταρίες...; **e**khete batar**ee**-es...?
for this camera/ camcorder	γι'αυτή τη φωτογραφική μηχανή/βιντεοκάμερα yaft**ee** tee fotoghrafeek**ee** meekhan**ee**/video**ca**mera
Can you develop this film?	Μπορείτε να εμφανίσετε αυτό το φιλμ; bor**ee**te na emfan**ee**sete aft**o** to feelm?
How much will it be?	Πόσο θα κοστίσει; p**o**so tha kost**ee**see?
Would you take a picture of us, please?	Μπορείτε να μας τραβήξετε μία φωτογραφία, παρακαλώ; bor**ee**te na mas trav**ee**ksete m**ee**a fotoghraf**ee**a parakal**o**?

> **Numbers** (p 109)

Leisure

Sightseeing and tourist office

• •

The Greek Tourist Organisation (EOT) has offices
in the larger towns in Greece, as does the Cyprus
Tourism Organisation (KOT) in Cyprus. If you are
looking for somewhere to stay, they should have
details of hotels and campsites as well as of
transport, local sights and events.

Where is the tourist office?	Πού είναι το τουριστικό γραφείο;
	poo **ee**ne to tooreesteek**o** ghraf**ee**o?
What can we visit in the area?	Τι μπορούμε να δούμε σ' αυτή την περιοχή;
	tee bor**oo**me na dh**oo**me saft**ee** teen pereeokh**ee**?
When can we visit...?	Πότε μπορούμε να επισκεφθούμε...;
	p**o**te bor**oo**me na epeeskefth**oo**me...?

72

the church	**την εκκλησία**
	teen eklees**ee**a
the museum	**το μουσείο**
	to moos**ee**o
Are there any excursions?	**Γίνονται εκδρομές;**
	y**ee**nonte ekdhrom**e**s?
How much does the entrance cost?	**Πόσο κάνει η είσοδος;**
	p**o**so k**a**nee ee **ee**sodhos?
Are there any reductions for...?	**Γίνεται έκπτωση για...;**
	y**ee**nete **e**kptosee ya...?
children	**παιδιά**
	pedhy**a**
students	**φοιτητές**
	feeteet**e**s
senior citizens	**ηλικιωμένους**
	eeleekeeom**e**noos

> **Maps and guides** (p 69) > **Leisure** (p 75)

Entertainment

• •

Details of entertainments can be found in newspapers. Local tourist offices will also have details of local festivals. **ATHINORAMA**, a listings magazine, is available in English from kiosks in Athens.

What is there to do in the evenings?	Τι μπορεί να κάνει κανείς τα βράδυα; tee boree na kanee kanees ta vradheea?
Do you know what events are on this week?	Ξέρετε τι εκδηλώσεις γίνονται αυτή τη βδομάδα; kserete tee ekdheelosees yeenonde aftee tee vdhomadha?
Is there anything for children?	Υπάρχει τίποτε για παιδιά; eeparkhee teepote ya pedhya?

YOU MAY HEAR...

Η είσοδος περιλαμβάνει και ένα ποτό ee eesodhos pereelamvanee ke ena poto	The entry fee includes one free drink

> **Music** (p 76) > **Theatre/opera** (p 78)

Leisure

Leisure/interests

• •

Where can I go...?	**Πού μπορώ να πάω για...;**
	p**oo** bor**o** na p**a**o ya...?
fishing	**ψάρεμα**
	ps**a**rema
Is there a swimming pool?	**Υπάρχει πισίνα;**
	eep**a**rkhee pees**ee**na?
When can we hire bikes?	**Πότε μπορούμε να νοικιάσουμε ποδήλατα;**
	p**o**te bor**oo**me na neeky**a**soome podh**ee**lata?
How much is it...?	**Πόσο κοστίζει...;**
	p**o**so kost**ee**zee...?
per hour	**την ώρα**
	teen **o**ra
per day	**τη μέρα**
	tee m**e**ra

> **Beach** (p 77) > **Sport** (p 80) > **Walking** (p 81)

Leisure/interests

Music

· ·

Leisure

Are there any good concerts on?	Υπάρχει καμία καλή συναυλία; eep**a**rkhee kam**ee**a kal**ee** seenavl**ee**a?
Where can I hear some Greek music and songs?	Πού μπορώ να ακούσω ελληνική μουσική και τραγούδια; p**oo** bor**o** na ak**oo**so eleeneek**ee** mooseek**ee** ke tragh**oo**dhya?

76

Beach

. . . .

Is there a good beach near here?	Υπάρχει μία καλή παραλία εδώ κοντά;
	eeparkhee meea kalee paraleea edho konda?
sandy	με άμμο
	me amo
Can I get there...?	Μπορώ να πάω εκεί..;
	boro na pao ekee...?
by bus	με λεωφορείο
	me leoforeeo
by car	με αυτοκίνητο
	me aftokeeneeto
Does it have...?	Έχει...;
	ekhee...?
toilets	τουαλέτες
	tooaletes
a restaurant	εστιατόριο
	esteeatoreeo
Can I hire...?	Μπορώ να νοικιάσω...;
	boro na neekyaso...?
a deckchair	μια ξαπλώστρα
	mya ksaplostra
an umbrella	μια ομπρέλα
	mya ombrela

Beach

> **Making friends** (p 23) > **Leisure** (p 75)

Theatre/opera

Classical Greek plays are performed at the Theatre of Herod Atticus at the foot of the Acropolis in Athens, at the theatre at Epidavros in the Peloponnese and elsewhere. It helps enormously if you buy an English translation of the play from a Greek bookshop and read it first to familiarise yourself with the plot. Hint: if you are planning to spend several hours sitting on a stone seat, take a cushion.

Leisure

What's on at the theatre?	Τι παίζει το θέατρο;
	tee pezee to theatro?
How do we get to the theatre?	Πώς θα πάμε στο θέατρο;
	pos tha pame sto theatro?
What prices are the tickets?	Τι τιμές έχουν τα εισιτήρια;
	tee teemes ekhoon ta eeseeteereea?
Two tickets...	Δύο εισιτήρια...
	dheeo eeseeteereea...
for tonight	για απόψε
	ya apopse
for tomorrow night	για αύριο βράδυ
	ya avreeo vradhee
When does the performance begin?	Πότε αρχίζει η παράσταση;
	pote arkheezee ee parastasee?

| When does the performance end? | Πότε τελειώνει η παράσταση; |
| | pote teleeonee ee parastasee? |

Television

●●●●●●●●●●●●●●●●●●●●●●●●●●●●●●

Where is the television/ the video?	Πού είναι η τηλεόραση/ το βίντεο;
	poo eene ee teeleorasee/ to veedeo?
How do you switch it on?	Από πού ανάβει;
	apo poo anavee?
Please lower the volume	Χαμηλώνετε παρακαλώ τη φωνή
	khameelonete parakalo tee fonee
May I turn the volume up?	Μπορώ να δυναμώσω τη φωνή;
	boro na dheenamoso tee fonee?
When is the news?	Πότε έχει ειδήσεις;
	pote ekhee eedheesees?
Do you have any English-language channels?	Έχετε αγγλόφωνα κανάλια;
	ekhete anglofona kanalya?

Sport

....

Where can I...?	**Πού μπορώ να...;**
	poo boro na...?
play tennis	**παίξω τένις**
	pekso tenees
go swimming	**κολυμπήσω**
	koleembeeso
go jogging	**κάνω τζόκινγκ**
	kano jogging
go for a walk	**κάνω μία βόλτα**
	kano meea volta
How much is it per hour?	**Πόσο κοστίζει την ώρα;**
	poso kosteezee teen ora?
Can I hire...?	**Μπορώ να νοικιάσω...;**
	boro na neekyaso...?
rackets	**ρακέτες**
	raketes

Walking

....

Are there any guided walks?	Γίνονται καθόλου οργανωμένοι περίπατοι;
	y**ee**nonte kath**o**loo orghanom**e**nee per**ee**patee?
Are there any special walking routes?	Υπάρχουν κάποιες ειδικές διαδρομές περιπάτου;
	eep**a**rkhoon k**a**pee-es eedheek**e**s dheeadhrom**e**s pereep**a**too?
How many kilometres is the walk?	Πόσα χιλιόμετρα είναι ο περίπατος;
	p**o**sa kheely**o**metra **ee**ne o per**ee**patos?
We'd like to go mountain climbing	Θα θέλαμε να κάνουμε ορειβασία
	tha th**e**lame na k**a**noome oreevas**ee**a

> **Maps and guides** (p 69)

Communications

Telephone and mobile

To phone Greece from the UK, the international code is **00 30** followed by the Greek area code, e.g. Athens **210**, and the phone number you require. For Cyprus, dial **00 357** followed by the Cyprus area code, e.g. Nicosia **2**, Limassol **5**, and the phone number.

FACE TO FACE

A Παρακαλώ/Ναι
parakal**o**/Ne
Hello

B Θα ήθελα να μιλήσω στον/στην…
tha **ee**thela na meel**ee**so ston/steen…
I'd like to speak to…

A Ποιός είστε;
py**o**s **ee**ste?
Who's calling?

B Είμαι η Μαρία
eeme ee Mar**i**a
It's Maria

A Ένα λεπτό…/Περιμένετε, παρακαλώ
ena lept**o**…/pereem**e**nete, parakal**o**
Just a moment…/Hold on, please

I want to make a phone call	Θέλω να κάνω ένα τηλεφώνημα th**e**lo na k**a**no **e**na teelef**o**neema
Where can I buy a phonecard?	Πού μπορώ να αγοράσω μία τηλεκάρτα; poo bor**o** na aghor**a**so m**ee**a teelek**a**rta?
A phonecard, please	Μία τηλεκάρτα, παρακαλώ m**ee**a teelek**a**rta, parakal**o**
Do you have a mobile?	Έχετε κινητό (τηλέφωνο); **e**khete keeneet**o** (teel**e**fono)?
What is the number of your mobile?	Ποιός είναι ο αριθμός του κινητού σας (τηλεφώνου); py**o**s **ee**ne o areethm**o**s too keeneet**oo** sas (teelef**o**noo)?
My mobile number is…	Ο αριθμός του κινητού μου (τηλεφώνου) είναι… o areethm**o**s too keeneet**oo** moo (teelef**o**noo) **ee**ne…

Telephone and mobile

83

Mr...	Τον κύριο...
	ton k**ee**reeo...
Mrs/Ms...,	Την κυρία..., παρακαλώ
please	teen keer**ee**a..., parakal**o**
Extension	εσωτερική γραμμή
number	esotereek**ee** ghram**ee**

YOU MAY HEAR...	
Πήρατε λάθος αριθμό p**ee**rate l**a**thos areethm**o**	You've got the wrong number
Αφήστε το μήνυμά σας μετά από το χαρακτηριστικό ήχο af**ee**ste to m**ee**neem**a** sas met**a** ap**o** to kharakteereesteek**o ee**kho	Leave a message after the tone
Παρακαλούμε να κλείσετε τα κινητά τηλέφωνα parakal**oo**me na kl**ee**sete ta keeneet**a** teel**e**fona	Please switch off all mobiles

E-mail

●●●●●●●●●●●●●●●●●●●●●●●●●●●●●●●●●●●●●●

Although you will hear the English word e-mail
used, the proper Greek term for e-mail address is
η ηλεκτρονική διεύθυνση (ee eelektroneek**ee**
dhee-**e**ftheensee).

Do you have e-mail?	Έχετε e-mail; **e**khete e-mail?
How do you spell it?	Πώς γράφεται; p**o**s ghr**a**fete?
Did you get my e-mail?	Πήρατε το e-mail μου; p**ee**rate to e-mail moo?
My e-mail address is...	Η e-mail διεύθυνσή μου είναι... ee e-mail dhee-**e**ftheens**ee** moo **ee**ne...

Internet

● ●

It is usually easy to find an internet café where you
can check your e-mail messages, etc. National and
local tourist information can also be accessed via
the internet. Greek websites have the suffix .gr.

Are there any internet cafés here?	**Υπάρχουν internet café στην περιοχή;** ee**pa**rkhoon internet kaf**e** steen pereeokh**ee**?
How much does it cost...?	**Πόσο κοστίζει...;** p**o**so kost**ee**zee...?
for one hour	**για μια ώρα** ya mya **o**ra

Fax

To fax Greece from the UK, the international code is **00 30** followed by the Greek area code, e.g. Athens **210**, and the fax number. For Cyprus, dial **00 357** followed by the Cyprus area code, e.g. Nicosia **2**, Limassol **5**, and the fax number.

Addressing a fax

ΑΠΟ	from
ΥΠ' ΟΨΙΝ	for the attention of
ΗΜΕΡΟΜΗΝΙΑ	date
ΘΕΜΑ	re

Do you have a fax?	**Έχετε φαξ;** **e**khete fax?
What is your fax number?	**Ποιός είναι ο αριθμός του φαξ σας;** py**o**s **ee**ne o areethm**o**s too fax sas?
I want to send a fax	**Θέλω να στείλω ένα φαξ** th**e**lo na st**ee**lo **e**na fax

Practicalities

Money

Banks in Greece and Cyprus are generally open only during the morning (Greece: 8.30 am–1 pm, Cyprus 8.30 am–12 noon), although in tourist areas some may open outside these hours.

ΤΡΑΠΕΖΑ trapeza	bank
ΠΙΣΤΩΤΙΚΕΣ ΚΑΡΤΕΣ peestoteekes kartes	credit cards

Where can I change some money?	Πού μπορώ να αλλάξω χρήματα;
	poo boro na alakso khreemata?
Where is the nearest bank?	Πού είναι η κοντινότερη τράπεζα;
	poo eene ee kondeenoteree trapeza?
I want to change these traveller's cheques	Θέλω να αλλάξω αυτές τις ταξιδιωτικές επιταγές
	thelo na alakso aftes tees takseedhyoteekes epeetayes

| When does the bank open? | Πότε ανοίγει η τράπεζα;
pote an**ee**yee ee tra**pe**za? |
| When does the bank close? | Πότε κλείνει η τράπεζα;
p**o**te kl**ee**nee ee tr**a**peza? |

Paying

....

ευρώ	evr**o**	euro
λεπτά	lept**a**	cents
ΛΟΓΑΡΙΑΣΜΟΣ loghareeasm**o**s		bill
ΤΑΜΕΙΟ	tam**ee**o	cash desk
ΤΙΜΟΛΟΓΙΟ	teemol**o**yeeo	invoice
ΑΠΟΔΕΙΞΗ	ap**o**dheeksee	receipt

How much is it?	Πόσο κάνει; p**o**so k**a**nee?
Can I pay...?	Μπορώ να πληρώσω…; bor**o** na pleer**o**so…?
by credit card	με πιστωτική κάρτα me peestoteek**ee** k**a**rta
by cheque	με τσεκ me tsek
Do you take credit cards?	Παίρνετε πιστωτικές κάρτες; p**e**rnete peestoteek**e**s k**a**rtes?

Put it on my bill	Βάλτε το στο λογαριασμό μου
	valte to sto logharyasmo moo
I need a receipt	Χρειάζομαι απόδειξη
	khreeazome apodheeksee
Do I pay in advance?	Προπληρώνω;
	propleerono?
Where do I pay?	Πού πληρώνω;
	poo pleerono?

Luggage

My luggage hasn't arrived	Οι αποσκευές μου δεν έφτασαν
	ee aposkeves moo dhen eftasan
My suitcase has arrived damaged	Η βαλίτσα μου έφτασε χαλασμένη
	ee valeetsa moo eftase khalasmenee
Can I leave my luggage here?	Μπορώ να αφήσω εδώ τις αποσκευές μου;
	boro na afeeso edho tees aposkeves moo?

Μπορείτε να τις αφήσετε εδώ μέχρι τις 6 η ώρα bor**ee**te na tees af**ee**sete edh**o** m**e**khree tees **e**ksee ee **o**ra	You may leave it here until 6 o'clock

Repairs

....

This is broken	Έσπασε αυτό **e**spase aft**o**
Where can I get this repaired?	Πού θα μου το επισκευάσουν; poo tha moo to epeeskev**a**soon?
Is it worth repairing?	Αξίζει τον κόπο να επισκευαστεί; aks**ee**zee ton k**o**po na epeeskevast**ee**?
Can you repair...?	Μπορείτε να επισκευάσετε...; bor**ee**te na epeeskev**a**sete...?
these shoes	αυτά τα παπούτσια aft**a** ta pap**oo**tsya
my watch	το ρολόι μου o rol**oee** moo

Laundry

You can get clothes washed or dry-cleaned at laundries in Greece. Self-service launderettes do not exist.

ΚΑΘΑΡΙΣΤΗΡΙΟ kathareest**ee**reeo	dry-cleaner's

Where can I do some washing?	Πού μπορώ να πλύνω μερικά ρούχα; poo bor**o** na pl**ee**no mereek**a** r**oo**kha?
Is there a dry-cleaner's near here?	Υπάρχει καθαριστήριο εδώ κοντά; eep**a**rkhee kathareest**ee**reeo edh**o** kond**a**?

Complaints

This doesn't work	Δε δουλεύει αυτό dhe dhoolevee aft**o**
The ... doesn't work	ο/η/το ... δε δουλεύει o/ee/to ... dhe dhool**e**vee
The ... don't work	οι/τα ... δε δουλεύουν ee/ta ... dhe dhool**e**voon

lights	τα φώτα
	ta fota
heating	η θέρμανση
	ee thermansee
air conditioning	ο κλιματισμός
	o kleemateesmos
This is dirty	Αυτό είναι βρώμικο
	afto eene vromeeko
There's a problem with the room	Υπάρχει πρόβλημα με το δωμάτιο
	eeparkhee provleema me to dhomateeo
It's noisy	Έχει θόρυβο
	ekhee thoreevo
I want a refund	Θέλω τα χρήματά μου πίσω
	thelo ta khreemata moo peeso

Problems

. . . .

Can you help me?	Μπορείτε να με βοηθήσετε;
	boreete na me voeetheesete?
I only speak a little Greek	Μιλάω μόνο λίγα ελληνικά
	meelao mono leegha eleeneeka
Does anyone here speak English?	Μιλά κανείς εδώ αγγλικά;
	meela kanees edho angleeka?

Problems

I would like to speak to whoever is in charge	Θα ήθελα να μιλήσω στον υπεύθυνο
	tha **ee**thela na meel**ee**so ston eep**e**ftheeno
I'm lost	Έχω χαθεί
	ekho khath**ee**
How do I get to...?	Πώς θα πάω στο...;
	p**o**s tha p**a**o sto...?
I've missed...	Έχασα...
	ekhasa...
my bus	το λεωφορείο μου
	to leofor**ee**o moo
my plane	το αεροπλάνο μου
	to aeropl**a**no moo
Can you show me how this works?	Μπορείτε να μου δείξετε πώς δουλεύει αυτό;
	bor**ee**te na moo dh**ee**ksete pos dhool**e**vee aft**o**?
I have lost my purse	Έχασα το πορτοφόλι μου
	ekhasa to portof**o**lee moo
I need to get to...	Πρέπει να φτάσω στο...
	pr**e**pee na ft**a**so sto...

Emergencies

The emergency numbers in Greece (for Athens) are POLICE **100**, AMBULANCE **166** and FIRE **199**. In Cyprus the emergency number for all these services is **199**.

ΑΣΤΥΝΟΜΙΑ asteenom**ee**a	police
ΑΣΘΕΝΟΦΟΡΟ asthenof**o**ro	ambulance
ΠΥΡΟΣΒΕΣΤΙΚΗ peerosvesteek**ee**	fire brigade

Help!	**Βοήθεια!** vo**ee**theea!
Fire!	**Φωτιά!** foty**a**!
Can you help me?	**Μπορείτε να με βοηθήσετε;** bor**ee**te na me voeeth**ee**sete?
There's been an accident!	**Έγινε ατύχημα!** **e**yeene at**ee**kheema!
Someone is injured	**Κάποιος τραυματίστηκε** k**a**pyos travmat**ee**steeke
Someone has been knocked down by a car	**Κάποιον χτύπησε ένα αυτοκίνητο** k**a**pyon kht**ee**peese **e**na aftok**ee**neeto

Call...	Φωνάξτε...
	fonakste...
the police	την αστυνομία
	teen asteenomeea
an ambulance	ένα ασθενοφόρο
	ena asthenoforo
please	παρακαλώ
	parakalo
Where is the police station?	Πού είναι το αστυνομικό τμήμα;
	poo eene to asteenomeeko tmeema?
I've been robbed	Με έκλεψαν
	me eklepsan
I want to report a theft	Θέλω να αναφέρω μια κλοπή
	thelo na anafero mya klopee
My car has been stolen	Μου έκλεψαν το αυτοκίνητο
	moo eklepsan to aftokeeneeto
Someone's stolen my...	Κάποιος μου έκλεψε...
	kapyos moo eklepse...
...bag	...την τσάντα
	...teen tsanda
...traveller's cheques	...τις ταξιδιωτικές επιταγές
	...tees takseedheeoteekes epeeta-yes

My car has been broken into	Μου παραβίασαν το αυτοκίνητο
	moo paravee**asan to aftok**ee**neeto
I've been attacked	Μου επιτέθηκαν
	moo epeet**e**theekan
I've been raped	Με βίασαν
	me v**ee**asan
I want to speak to a policewoman	Θέλω να μιλήσω σε γυναίκα αστυνομικό
	th**e**lo na meel**ee**so se yeen**e**ka asteenomeek**o**
I need to make an urgent telephone call	Πρέπει να κάνω ένα επείγον τηλεφώνημα
	pr**e**pee na k**a**no **e**na ep**ee**ghon teelef**o**neema
I need a report for my insurance	Θέλω μια αναφορά για την ασφαλιστική μου εταιρεία
	th**e**lo mya anafor**a** ya teen asfaleesteek**ee** moo eter**ee**a
I didn't know the speed limit	Δεν ήξερα το όριο ταχύτητας
	dhen **ee**ksera to **o**reeo takh**ee**teetas
I'm very sorry	Λυπάμαι πολύ
	leep**a**me pol**ee**

How much is the fine?	Πόσο είναι το πρόστιμο;
	poso **ee**ne to pr**o**steemo?
Where do I pay it?	Πού θα το πληρώσω;
	poo tha to pleer**o**so?

| Περάσατε με κόκκινο per**a**sate me k**o**keeno | You went through a red light |

Health

Pharmacy

....

| ΦΑΡΜΑΚΕΙΟ | farmak**ee**o | pharmacy/chemist |
| ΣΥΝΤΑΓΗ | seenday**ee** | prescription |

I don't feel well	**Δεν αισθάνομαι καλά**
	dhen esth**a**nome kal**a**
Have you something for...?	**Έχετε τίποτε για...;**
	ekhete t**ee**pote ya...?
sunburn	**τα εγκαύματα**
	ta eng**a**vmata
travel sickness	**τη ναυτία**
	tee naft**ee**a
diarrhoea	**τη διάρροια**
	tee dhee**a**reea
Is it safe for children?	**Είναι ασφαλές για παιδιά;**
	eene asfal**e**s ya pedy**a**?
How much should I give?	**Πόσο πρέπει να δώσω;**
	p**o**so pr**e**pee na dh**o**so?

Να το παίρνετε τρεις φορές την ημέρα πριν/με/μετά το φαγητό na to pernete trees fores teen eemera preen/me/meta to fayeeto	Take it three times a day before/with/after meals

Doctor

....

ΝΟΣΟΚΟΜΕΙΟ nosokomeeo	hospital

FACE TO FACE

A Δεν νιώθω καλά
then neeotho kala
I don't feel very well

B Έχετε πυρετό;
ekhete peereto?
Do you have a temperature?

A Όχι, πονάω εδώ...
okhi, ponao edho...
No, I have a pain here...

Health

I need a doctor	**Χρειάζομαι γιατρό**
	khree**a**zome yatr**o**
My son is ill	**Ο γιος μου είναι άρρωστος**
	o yos moo **ee**ne **a**rostos
My daughter is ill	**Η κόρη μου είναι άρρωστη**
	ee k**o**ree moo **ee**ne **a**rostee
I'm pregnant	**Είμαι έγγυος**
	eeme **e**ngeeos
I'm diabetic	**Είμαι διαβητικός(-ή)**
	eeme dheeaveeteek-**o**s(-ee)
I'm allergic	**Έχω αλλεργία στην**
to penicillin	**πενικιλλίνη**
	ekho alery**ee**a steen
	peneekeel**ee**nee
My blood	**Η ομάδα αίματός μου**
group is...	**είναι...**
	ee om**a**dha **e**mat**o**s moo **ee**ne...
I've been stung	**κάτι με τσίμπησε**
by something	k**a**tee me ts**ee**mbeese
Will he/she	**Πρέπει να μπει στο**
have to go	**νοσοκομείο;**
to hospital?	pr**e**pee na bee sto nosokom**ee**o?
I need a receipt	**Χρειάζομαι απόδειξη για**
for the	**την ασφαλιστική μου**
insurance	**εταιρεία**
	khree**a**zome ap**o**dheeksee ya teen
	asfaleesteek**ee** moo eter**ee**a

Θα πρέπει να μπείτε στο νοσοκομείο tha prepee na beete sto nosokomeeo	You will have to go into hospital
Δεν είναι σοβαρό dhen eene sovaro	It's not serious

Dentist

I need a dentist	Χρειάζομαι οδοντίατρο khreeazome odhondeeatro
He/She has toothache	Έχει πονόδοντο ekhee ponodhondo
Can you do a temporary filling?	Μπορείτε να κάνετε προσωρινό σφράγισμα; boreete na kanete prosoreeno sfra-yeesma?
It hurts (me)	Με πονάει me ponaee
Can you give me something for the pain?	Μπορείτε να μου δώσετε κάτι για τον πόνο; boreete na moo dhosete katee ya ton pono?
How much will it be?	Πόσο θα κοστίσει; poso tha kosteesee?

| I need a receipt for my insurance | Χρειάζομαι απόδειξη για την ασφαλιστική μου εταιρεία |
| | khree**a**zome ap**o**dheeksee ya teen asfaleesteek**ee** moo eter**ee**a |

| Πρέπει να βγει prep**ee** na vyee | It has to come out |

Dentist

Different types of travellers

Disabled travellers

• •

Facilities for the disabled are not as widely available in Greece and Cyprus as in the UK, although they are improving. It is worth checking with individual hotels etc. prior to booking. The new underground in Athens has superb facilities for the disabled.

What facilities do you have for disabled people?	Τι ευκολίες έχετε για άτομα με ειδικές ανάγκες; tee efkol**ee**-es **e**khete ya **a**toma me eedheek**e**s an**a**nges?
Are there any toilets for the disabled?	Υπάρχουν τουαλέτες για άτομα με ειδικές ανάγκες; eep**a**rkhoon tooal**e**tes ya **a**toma me eedheek**e**s an**a**nges?
Do you have any bedrooms on the ground floor?	Έχετε υπνοδωμάτια στο ισόγειο; **e**khete eepnodhom**a**teea sto ees**o**yeeo?
Is there a lift?	Υπάρχει ασανσέρ; eep**a**rkhee asans**e**r?

Where is the lift?	Πού είναι το ασανσέρ;
	poo eene to asanser?
How many stairs are there?	Πόσες σκάλες υπάρχουν;
	poses skales eeparkhoon?
Do you have wheelchairs?	Έχετε καρότσια;
	ekhete karotsya?
Can you visit ... in a wheelchair?	Μπορεί κανείς να επισκεφτεί ... με καρότσι;
	boree kanees na epeeskeftee ... me karotsee?
Where is the wheelchair-accessible entrance?	Πού είναι η είσοδος με πρόσβαση για τα καρότσια;
	poo eene ee eesodhos me prosvasee ya ta karotsya?
Is there a reduction for disabled people?	Γίνεται έκπτωση στα άτομα με ειδικές ανάγκες;
	yeenete ekptosee sta atoma me eedheekes ananges?

With kids

• •

A child's ticket	Ένα παιδικό εισιτήριο
	ena pedhee**ko** eeseet**ee**reeo
He/She is ...	είναι ... χρονών
years old	**ee**ne ... khron**on**
Is there a	Υπάρχει ειδική τιμή για
reduction for	παιδιά;
children?	eep**ar**khee eedheek**ee** teem**ee** ya
	pedhy**a**?
Is there a	Υπάρχει παιδικό μενού;
children's	eep**ar**khee pedhee**ko** men**oo**?
menu?	
Have you...?	Έχετε...;
	ekhete...?
a high chair	μία παιδική καρέκλα
	m**ee**a pedheek**ee** kar**e**kla
a cot	ένα παιδικό κρεββάτι
	ena pedhee**ko** krev**a**tee
Is it ok to bring	Υπάρχει πρόβλημα αν
children?	φέρουμε τα παιδιά;
	eep**ar**khee pr**o**vleema an f**e**roome
	ta pedhy**a**?
Do you have	Έχετε παιδιά;
children?	**e**khete pedhy**a**?

Reference

Measurements and quantities

••

Liquids

1/2 litre of...	**μισό λίτρο**...
	mees**o lee**tro...
a litre of...	**ένα λίτρο**...
	ena **lee**tro...
a bottle of...	**ένα μπουκάλι**...
	ena book**a**lee...
a glass of...	**ένα ποτήρι**...
	ena pot**ee**ree...

Weights

••••••••••••••

100 grams	**εκατό γραμμάρια**
	ekat**o** ghram**a**reea
1/2 kilo of...	**μισό κιλό**...
(500 g)	mees**o** keel**o**...
a kilo of...	**ένα κιλό**...
(1000 g)	**e**na keel**o**...

Food

a slice of...	**μια φέτα...**
	mya **fe**ta...
a portion of...	**μια μερίδα...**
	mya mer**ee**dha...
a box of...	**ένα κουτί...**
	ena koot**ee**...
a packet of...	**ένα πακέτο...**
	ena pak**e**to...
a tin of...	**μια κονσέρβα...**
	mya kons**e**rva...
a jar of...	**ένα βάζο...**
	ena v**a**zo...

Miscellaneous

10 euros	**δέκα ευρώ**
	dh**e**ka evr**o**
20 cents	**είκοσι λεπτά**
	eekosee lept**a**
a third	**ένα τρίτο**
	ena tr**ee**to
a quarter	**ένα τέταρτο**
	ena t**e**tarto
ten per cent	**δέκα τοις εκατό**
	dh**e**ka tees ekat**o**
more...	**περισσότερο...**
	perees**o**tero...

less...	**λιγότερο...**
	leegh**o**tero...
enough	**αρκετό**
	arket**o**
double	**διπλό**
	dheepl**o**
twice	**διπλάσιο**
	dheepl**a**seeo
three times	**τριπλάσιο**
	treepl**a**seeo

Numbers

. . . .

0	**μηδέν** meedh**e**n
1	**ένα e**na
2	**δύο** dh**ee**o
3	**τρία** tr**ee**a
4	**τέσσερα** t**e**sera
5	**πέντε** p**e**nde
6	**έξι e**ksee
7	**εφτά** eft**a**
8	**οχτώ** okht**o**
9	**εννιά** eny**a**
10	**δέκα** dh**e**ka
11	**έντεκα e**ndeka
12	**δώδεκα** dh**o**dheka
13	**δεκατρία** dhekatr**ee**a

14	**δεκατέσσερα** dhekatesera
15	**δεκαπέντε** dhekapende
16	**δεκαέξι** dhekaeksee
17	**δεκαεφτά** dhekaefta
18	**δεκαοχτώ** dhekaokhto
19	**δεκαεννιά** dhekaenya
20	**είκοσι** eekosee
21	**είκοσι ένα** eekosee ena
22	**είκοσι δύο** eekosee dheeo
30	**τριάντα** treeanda
40	**σαράντα** saranda
50	**πενήντα** peneenda
60	**εξήντα** ekseenda
70	**εβδομήντα** evdhomeenda
80	**ογδόντα** oghdhonda
90	**ενενήντα** eneneenda
100	**εκατό** ekato
110	**εκατόν δέκα** ekaton dheka
500	**πεντακόσια** pendakosya
1,000	**χίλια** kheelya
2,000	**δύο χιλιάδες** dheeo kheelyadhes
1 million	**ένα εκατομμύριο** ena ekatomeereeo

1st	**πρώτος**	6th	**έκτος**
	protos		ektos
2nd	**δεύτερος**	7th	**έβδομος**
	dhefteros		evdhomos
3rd	**τρίτος**	8th	**όγδοος**
	treetos		oghdho-os
4th	**τέταρτος**	9th	**ένατος**
	tetartos		enatos
5th	**πέμπτος**	10th	**δέκατος**
	pemptos		dhekatos

Days and months

Days

Monday	**Δευτέρα**	dheftera
Tuesday	**Τρίτη**	treetee
Wednesday	**Τετάρτη**	tetartee
Thursday	**Πέμπτη**	pemptee
Friday	**Παρασκευή**	paraskevee
Saturday	**Σάββατο**	savato
Sunday	**Κυριακή**	keeryakee

Months

January	**Ιανουάριος**	eeanoo**a**reeos
February	**Φεβρουάριος**	fevroo**a**reeos
March	**Μάρτιος**	m**a**rteeos
April	**Απρίλιος**	apr**ee**leeos
May	**Μάιος**	m**a**eeos
June	**Ιούνιος**	ee**oo**neeos
July	**Ιούλιος**	ee**oo**leeos
August	**Αύγουστος**	**av**ghoostos
September	**Σεπτέμβριος**	sept**e**mvreeos
October	**Οκτώβριος**	okt**o**vreeos
November	**Νοέμβριος**	no**e**mvreeos
December	**Δεκέμβριος**	dhek**e**mvreeos

Seasons

spring	**Άνοιξη**	**a**neeksee
summer	**Καλοκαίρι**	kalok**e**ree
autumn	**Φθινόπωρο**	ftheen**o**poro
winter	**Χειμώνας**	kheem**o**nas

What's the date?	**Τι ημερομηνία έχουμε;**
	tee eemeromeen**ee**a **e**khoome?
It's the 5th of August 2007	**Είναι η 5η Αυγούστου 2007**
	eene ee p**e**mptee avgh**oo**stoo dh**ee**o kheelee**a**des eft**a**

on Saturday	**το Σάββατο**
	to s**a**vato
on Saturdays	**τα Σάββατα**
	ta s**a**vata
this Saturday	**αυτό το Σάββατο**
	aft**o** to s**a**vato
next Saturday	**το επόμενο Σάββατο**
	to ep**o**meno s**a**vato
last Saturday	**το περασμένο Σάββατο**
	to perasm**e**no s**a**vato
in June	**τον Ιούνιο**
	ton ee**oo**neeo
at the beginning of June	**στις αρχές Ιουνίου**
	stees arkh**e**s eeoon**ee**oo
at the end of June	**στα τέλη Ιουνίου**
	sta t**e**lee eeoon**ee**oo
before summer	**πριν από το καλοκαίρι**
	preen ap**o** to kalok**e**ree
during the summer	**μέσα στο καλοκαίρι**
	m**e**sa sto kalok**e**ree
after summer	**μετά το καλοκαίρι**
	met**a** to kalok**e**ree

Time

••

When telling the time in Greek, remember that the
hour comes first, then 'past' **και** (ke) or 'to' **παρά**
(par**a**) and finally the minutes, e.g. 8.10 **οκτώ και**
δέκα (okt**o** ke dh**e**ka) – ten past eight, 11.40
δώδεκα παρά είκοσι (dh**o**dheka par**a** **ee**kosee) –
twenty to twelve.

What time is it, please?	**Τι ώρα είναι, παρακαλώ;**
	tee **o**ra **e**ene, parakal**o**?
am	**πμ**
	preen to meseem**e**ree
pm	**μμ**
	met**a** to meseem**e**ree
It's...	**Είναι...**
	eene...
2 o'clock	**δύο η ώρα**
	dh**ee**o ee **o**ra
3 o'clock	**τρεις η ώρα**
	trees ee **o**ra
6 o'clock (etc.)	**έξι η ώρα**
	eksee ee **o**ra
It's 1 o'clock	**Είναι μία η ώρα**
	eene m**ee**a ee **o**ra
It's 1200	**Είναι δώδεκα**
	eene dh**o**dheka

midday	**το μεσημέρι**
	to meseemeree
midnight	**τα μεσάνυχτα**
	ta mesaneekhta
9	**εννέα**
	enea
9.10	**εννέα και δέκα**
	enea ke dheka
quarter past 9	**εννέα και τέταρτο**
	enea ke tetarto
9.20	**εννέα και είκοσι**
	enea ke eekosee
9.30	**εννέα και μισή**
	enea ke meesee
9.35	**εννέα και τριάντα πέντε**
	enea ke treeanta pente
quarter to 10	**δέκα παρά τέταρτο**
	dheka para tetarto
10 to 10	**δέκα παρά δέκα**
	dheka para dheka

Time phrases

....

When does it open/close?	**Πότε ανοίγει/κλείνει;** pote an**ee**yee/kl**ee**nee?
When does it begin/finish?	**Πότε αρχίζει/τελειώνει;** pote arkh**ee**zee/telee**o**nee?
at 3 o'clock	**στις τρεις η ώρα** stees trees ee **o**ra
before 3 o'clock	**πριν από τις τρεις** preen ap**o** tees trees
after 3 o'clock	**μετά τις τρεις** met**a** tees trees
today	**σήμερα** s**ee**mera
tonight	**απόψε** ap**o**pse
tomorrow	**αύριο** **av**reeo
yesterday	**χθες** khthes

Eating out

Eating places

ΜΠΑΡ (bar) Serves drinks and sometimes snacks.

ΚΑΦΕΤΕΡΙΑ (kaf**e**t**e**reea) Serves drinks, coffee, light meals, snacks.

ΤΑΒΕΡΝΑ (tav**e**rna) Either a traditional tavern or an establishment aimed at the tourist.

ΟΥΖΕΡΙ (oozer**ee**) A small bar serving ouzo and other traditional drinks. They may also serve mezedes.

ΣΟΥΒΛΑΤΖΙΔΙΚΟ (soovlatz**ee**dheeko) Take-aways selling mainly pork kebabs (soovl**a**kee) and chips.

ΚΑΦΕΝΕΙΟ (kafen**ee**o) Traditional coffee shop which is often a social centre for the men of a village.

ΕΣΤΙΑΤΟΡΙΟ (esteeatoreeo) Restaurant.

ΡΕΣΤΟΡΑΝ (restoran) Restaurants in tourist resorts usually start serving food from midday or 1 pm until late at night. Greeks tend to have a large meal for lunch between 1 and 3 pm. If going out for dinner, they tend to do so after 8 or 9 pm.

ΖΑΧΑΡΟΠΛΑΣΤΕΙΟ (zakharoplasteeo) Patisserie selling sweet Greek pastries either to take away or to eat on the premises. It will usually also serve coffee and soft drinks.

In a bar/café

If you ask for a coffee you are likely to be served a Greek (Turkish) coffee. If you like it sweet ask for **καφέ γλυκό** (kafe gleeko), medium sweet is **καφέ μέτριο** (kafe metreeo) and without sugar is **καφέ σκέτο** (kafe sketo). If you want an instant coffee you will need to ask for **ένα νεσκαφέ** (ena neskafe). A refreshing drink in the summer is iced coffee. Ask for **καφέ φραπέ** (kafe frape).

A Τί θα πάρετε;
tee tha **p**arete?
What will you have?

B Ένα τσάι με γάλα παρακαλώ
ena ts**a**ee me gh**a**la parakal**o**
A tea with milk, please

a cappuccino	ένα καπουτσίνο
	ena kapoots**ee**no
a beer	μία μπύρα
	m**ee**a b**ee**ra
an ouzo	ένα ούζο
	ena o**u**zo
...please	...παρακαλώ
	...parakal**o**
a tea...	ένα τσάι...
	ena ts**a**ee...
with lemon	με λεμόνι
	me lem**o**nee
without sugar	χωρίς ζάχαρη
	khor**ee**s z**a**kharee
for me	για μένα
	ya m**e**na
for her	γι' αυτήν
	yaft**ee**n
for him	γι' αυτόν
	yaft**o**n

119

for us	για μας
	ya mas
A bottle of	Ένα μπουκάλι
mineral water	εμφιαλωμένο νερό
	ena book**a**lee emfeealom**e**no
	ner**o**
sparkling	αεριούχο
	aeree**oo**kho
still	απλό
	apl**o**

Other drinks to try

ένα χυμό λεμονιού (**e**na kheem**o** lemony**oo**)
  a lemon juice

ένα χυμό πορτοκαλιού (**e**na kheem**o**
  portokaly**oo**) an orange juice

ένα ποτήρι ρετσίνα (**e**na pot**ee**ree rets**ee**na)
  a glass of retsina

ένα κονιάκ (**e**na kony**a**k) a brandy

ένα αναψυκτικό (**e**na anapseekteek**o**)
  a soft drink

In a restaurant

....

A Θα ήθελα ένα τραπέζι για ... άτομα
tha **ee**thela **e**na trap**e**zee ya ... **a**toma
I'd like to book a table for ... people

B Ναι, για πότε;
ne, ya p**o**te?
Yes, when for?

A για απόψε.../για αύριο βράδυ...
ya ap**o**pse.../ya **a**vreeo vr**a**dee...
For tonight.../For tomorrow night...

The menu, please	Τον κατάλογο, παρακαλώ	
	ton kat**a**logho, parakal**o**	
What is the dish of the day?	Ποιο είναι το πιάτο της ημέρας;	
	pyo **ee**ne to py**a**to tees eem**e**ras?	
Have you a set price menu?	Έχετε ένα προκαθορισμένο μενού;	
	ekhete **e**na prokathoreesm**e**no men**oo**?	
What is this?	Τι είναι αυτό;	
	tee **ee**ne aft**o**?	
I'll have this	Θα πάρω αυτό	
	tha p**a**ro aft**o**	
Excuse me!	Με συγχωρείτε!	
	me seenkhor**ee**te!	

In a restaurant

121

Please bring...	Παρακαλώ, φέρτε...
	parakal**o** f**e**rte...
more bread	κι άλλο ψωμί
	kee **a**lo psom**ee**
more water	κι άλλο νερό
	kee **a**lo ner**o**
another bottle	άλλο ένα μπουκάλι
	alo **e**na book**a**lee
the bill	το λογαριασμό
	to loghar**ee**asm**o**

Reading the menu

A Greek meal usually consists of one substantial main course, often with chips and salad, followed by a simple dessert such as fresh fruit. Bread is absolutely compulsory and Greeks often order a few side dishes to share.

Starters ΟΡΕΚΤΙΚΑ (orekteek**a**)

τζατζίκι (tzatz**ee**kee) yoghurt, cucumber, and garlic dip

ταραμοσαλάτα (taramosal**a**ta) dip made from fish roe

ελιές (ely**e**s) olives usually marinated in olive oil and garlic

γιαούρτι (ya**oo**rtee) yogurt

καλαμάρια (kalam**a**rya) sliced squid in batter

κεφτέδες (keft**e**dhes) meat balls

αγγουροντομάτα (angoorondom**a**ta) tomato and cucumber salad

φέτα (f**e**ta) feta cheese

χταπόδι (khtap**o**dhee) octopus

λουκάνικο (look**a**neeko) sausage

Greek dishes you might like to try

ντολμαδάκια (dolmadh**a**kya) stuffed vineleaves

πιπεριές γεμιστές (peepery**e**s yemeest**e**s) stuffed peppers

παστίτσιο (past**ee**tsyo) layers of pasta and minced meat, with a white sauce topping

μουσακάς (moossak**a**s) layers of aubergines and minced meat

γιουβέτσι (yoov**e**tsee) roast lamb with pasta

στιφάδο (steef**a**dho) beef and onions

Meat & poultry
ΚΡΕΑΣ ΚΑΙ ΠΟΥΛΕΡΙΚΑ (kr**e**as ke poolereek**a**)

μπριζόλα μοσχαρίσια (breez**o**la moskhar**ee**sya) beefsteak

μπριζόλα χοιρινή (breez**o**la kheereen**ee**) pork chop

σουβλάκι χοιρινό (soovlakee kheereeno)
  pork kebab
σουβλάκι αρνίσιο (soovlakee arneesyo)
  lamb kebab
παϊδάκια αρνίσια (paeedhakya arneesya)
  lamb chops
μοσχάρι ψητό (moskharee pseeto) roast beef
κοτόπουλο ψητό (kotopoolo pseeto) roast chicken

Fish ΨΑΡΙΑ (psareea)

γαρίδες (ghareedhes) prawns
μπαρμπούνι (barboonee) red mullet
λιθρίνι (leethreenee) grey mullet
αστακός (astakos) lobster
ξιφίας (kseefeeas) swordfish
γλώσσα (ghlosa) sole
σουπιές (soopyes) cuttlefish
λαβράκι (lavrakee) sea bass
τσιπούρα (tseepoora) sea bream

Eggs ΑΒΓΑ (avgha)

αβγά τηγανητά (avgha teeghaneeta) fried eggs
αβγά βραστά (avgha vrasta) boiled eggs
ομελέτα (omeleta) omelette
αβγά ζαμπόν (avgha zambon) ham and eggs

Vegetables ΛΑΧΑΝΙΚΑ (lakhaneeka)

μπάμιες (bamyes) okra, 'lady's fingers'
σπανάκι (spanakee) spinach
κολοκυθάκια (kolokeethakya) courgettes
μελιτζάνες (meleetzanes) aubergines, eggplant
καρότα (karota) carrots
αγγούρι (angooree) cucumber
ντομάτα (domata) tomato
μαρούλι (maroolee) lettuce
πατάτες (patates) potatoes
πατάτες τηγανητές (patates teeghaneetes)
  fried potatoes
πατάτες πουρέ (patates poore) mashed potatoes
πατάτες φούρνου (patates foornoo)
  roast potatoes

Fruit ΦΡΟΥΤΑ (froota)

σταφύλια (stafeelya) grapes
καρπούζι (karpoozee) watermelon
πεπόνι (peponee) melon
σύκα (seeka) figs
αχλάδια (akhladhya) pears
μήλα (meela) apples
κεράσια (kerasya) cherries
ροδάκινα (rodhakeena) peaches
βερίκοκα (vereekoka) apricots
φράουλες (fraooles) strawberries
μπανάνες (bananes) bananas

125

Although you may find some of these in restaurants, a Greek meal is rarely followed by a sweet dessert; it is more usual to have fresh fruit. The place to go for Greek sweets is the patisserie, **ΖΑΧΑΡΟΠΛΑΣΤΕΙΟ** (zakharoplast**ee**o).

πάστες (p**a**stes) slices of gateaux
μπακλαβάς (baklav**a**s) filo pastry filled with chopped almonds, in syrup
κανταΐφι (kanda**ee**fee) shredded pastry with a filling of chopped almonds, in syrup
παγωτό (paghot**o**) ice cream
γαλατομπούρεκο (ghalatob**oo**reko) filo pastry with a cream filling, in syrup
κομπόστα (kob**o**sta) stewed or tinned fruit

Vegetarian

....

You have to be a bit inventive! Although the Greeks eat a large number of vegetarian dishes in their own homes, they usually expect meat or fish when they go out to eat. There are some specialist vegetarian restaurants mainly catering for tourists.

Are there any vegetarian restaurants here?	Υπάρχουν καθόλου εστιατόρια για χορτοφάγους εδώ; eeparkhoon katholoo esteeatoreea ya khortofaghoos edho?
Do you have any vegetarian dishes?	Έχετε καθόλου φαγητά για χορτοφάγους; ekhete katholoo fa-yeeta ya khortofaghoos?
Which dishes have no meat/fish?	Ποια φαγητά δεν έχουν κρέας/ψάρι; pya fa-yeeta dhen ekhoon kreas/psaree?
What fish dishes do you have?	Τι φαγητά με ψάρια έχετε; tee fa-yeeta me psarya ekhete?
I don't like meat	Δεν μου αρέσει το κρέας dhen moo aresee to kreas
What do you recommend?	Τι προτείνετε; tee proteenete?

Possible dishes

μπάμιες (b**a**myes) okra or 'ladies' fingers', usually cooked in a tomato sauce

γίγαντες (y**ee**gantes) large butter beans, usually in tomato sauce with olive oil and herbs

μελιτζάνες (meleetz**a**nes) aubergines, usually stuffed

χωριάτικη σαλάτα (khory**a**teekee sal**a**ta) village salad, usually containing tomatoes, cucumber, olives, onions, feta cheese and a dressing of olive oil and lemon or vinegar

γεμιστά (yemeest**a**) tomatoes and peppers stuffed with rice and herbs

φασολάκια (fasol**a**kya) green beans simmered in olive oil and tomato

φακές (fak**e**s) lentil soup

Wines and spirits

The wine list, please	**Τον κατάλογο των κρασιών, παρακαλώ**
	ton kat**a**logho ton krasy**o**n, parakal**o**
Can you recommend a good wine?	**Μπορείτε να μας προτείνετε ένα καλό κρασί;**
	bor**ee**te na mas prot**ee**nete **e**na kal**o** kras**ee**?
A bottle...	**Ένα μπουκάλι...**
	ena book**a**lee...
A carafe...	**Μία καράφα...**
	m**ee**a kar**a**fa...
of (house) wine	**κρασί**
	kras**ee**
of red wine	**κόκκινο κρασί**
	k**o**keeno kras**ee**
of white wine	**λευκό κρασί**
	lefk**o** kras**ee**
of rosé wine	**κρασί ροζέ**
	kras**ee** roz**e**
of dry wine	**ξηρό κρασί**
	kseer**o** kras**ee**
of sweet wine	**γλυκό κρασί**
	ghleek**o** kras**ee**
of a local wine	**τοπικό κρασί**
	topeek**o** kras**ee**

Wines

Χατζημιχάλη (khadzeemeekhalee) a range of
   wines from N. Greece

Αχαία Κλάους (akhaya klaoos) a range of wines
   from the Peloponnese

Ζίτσα (zeetsa) sparkling white wine from Epirus

Αβέρωφ (averof) red wines from Epirus

Απέλια (apeleea) dry white wine

Δεμέστιχα (dhemesteekha) a dry wine, white or red

Κιτρό (keetro) a slightly sour white wine from Naxos

Κοκκινέλι (kokeenelee) a sweet red wine from Crete

Τσάνταλη (tsantalee) a selection of wines from
   Thrace and Macedonia

Αγιορείτικο (ayoreeteeko) wine made by monks
   on Mt Athos

Μάντικο (manteeko) a dry red wine from Crete

Μαυροδάφνη (mavrodhafnee) a sweet red dessert
   wine

Μόντε Χρήστος (monte khreestos) a sweet red
   wine from Cyprus

Μοσχάτο (moskhato) dark red dessert wine with
   muscatel flavour

Αφροδίτη (afrodheetee) a medium white wine
   from Cyprus

Ροδάμπελη (rodhabelee) a dry white wine

Σάμος (samos) traditional wine from the Aegean
   island of Samos

Νεμέας (nem**e**as) dry red wine from Nemea, Peloponnese

Beers

Beer is of the lager type and both bottled beer and draught are available. Some is brewed in Greece, some imported.

Spirits

κονιάκ (kony**a**k) brandy, ranked by a star system: the more stars, the better quality the brandy
ούζο (**oo**zo) an aniseed-flavoured colourless drink, drunk on its own or with water. When water is added it turns white
ρακή (rak**ee**) a clear strong spirit

Other drinks to try

ρετσίνα (rets**ee**na) a resinated white wine which can accompany a meal but can equally well be enjoyed on its own, especially well chilled or with soda, lemonade or Coke
κουμανταρία (koomantar**ee**a) very sweet dessert wine from Cyprus
φιλφάρ (feelf**a**r) an orange-flavoured liqueur from Cyprus

Menu reader

α **A**

αγγούρι ang**oo**ree cucumber

αγκινάρες ankeen**a**res artichokes

αεριούχο aeree**oo**kho fizzy, sparkling

αθερίνα ather**ee**na whitebait, usually fried

αλάτι al**a**tee salt

αλεύρι alevree flour

αμύγδαλα am**ee**ghdhala almonds

αρακάς arak**a**s peas

αρνί arn**ee** lamb

αρνί γιουβέτσι arn**ee** yoov**e**tsee roast lamb with small pasta

αρνί λεμονάτο arn**ee** lemon**a**to lamb braised in sauce with herbs and lemon juice

αρνί ψητό arn**ee** pseet**o** roast lamb

αστακός astak**o**s lobster (often served with lemon juice and olive oil)

άσπρο **a**spro white

άσπρο κρασί **a**spro kras**ee** white wine

αυγά avgh**a** eggs

αυγολέμονο avghol**e**mono egg and lemon soup

αφέλια af**e**leea pork in red wine with seasonings

αχλάδι akhl**a**dhee pear

β Β

βερίκοκο ver**ee**koko apricot

βλίτα vl**ee**ta wild greens (like spinach, eaten with olive oil and lemon)

βοδινό vodhe**e**no beef

βουτήματα voot**ee**mata biscuits to dip in coffee

βούτυρο v**oo**teero butter

βραδινό vradhe**e**no evening meal

βραστό vrast**o** boiled

γ Γ

γάλα gh**a**la milk

γαλακτομπούρικο ghalaktob**oo**reeko custard tart

γαρίδες ghar**ee**dhes shrimps; prawns

γαύρος gavros sardine-type fish (if salted: anchovy)

γίδα βραστή y**ee**da vrast**ee** goat soup

γεμιστά yemeest**a** stuffed vegetables

γιαούρτι ya**oo**rtee yoghurt

γιαούρτι με μέλι ya**oo**rtee me m**e**lee yoghurt with honey

γιαχνί yakhn**ee** cooked in tomato sauce and olive oil

γίγαντες y**ee**ghantes large butter beans

γιουβαρελάκια yoovarel**a**kya meatballs in lemon sauce

γλυκά ghleek**a** desserts

γλυκά κουταλιού ghleek**a** kootaly**oo** crystallized fruits in syrup

γλώσσα ghl**o**sa sole

γόπες gh**o**pes bogue, a type of fish

γραβιέρα ghravy**e**ra cheese resembling gruyère
γύρος y**ee**ros doner kebab

δ Δ
δείπνο dh**ee**pno dinner
δίπλες dh**ee**ples pastry with honey and walnuts

ε Ε
ελάχιστα ψημένο el**a**kheesta pseem**e**no rare (meat)
ελαιόλαδο ele**o**ladho olive oil
ελιές ely**e**s olives
ελιές τσακιστές ely**e**s tsakeest**e**s cracked green
  olives with coriander seeds and garlic (Cyprus)
εξοχικό eksokheek**o** stuffed pork or beef with
  vegetables and cheese

ζ Ζ
ζαμπόν zamb**o**n ham
ζάχαρη z**a**kharee sugar
ζεστή σοκολάτα zest**ee** sokol**a**ta hot chocolate
ζεστό zest**o** hot, warm

θ Θ
Θαλασσινά thalaseen**a** seafood
Θυμάρι theem**a**ree thyme

ι Ι
ιμάμ μπαϊλντί eem**a**m baeeld**ee** stuffed
  aubergines (eggplants)

κ K

κάβα k**a**va wine shop

καγιανάς με παστό κρέας kayan**a**s me past**o** kr**e**as salted pork with cheese, tomatoes and eggs

κακαβιά kakavy**a** fish soup

κακάο kak**ow** hot chocolate

καλαμάκι kalam**a**kee straw (for drinking); small skewer

καλαμάρια kalam**a**rya squid

καλοψημένο kalopseem**e**no well done (meat)

κανέλα kan**e**lla cinnamon

κάπαρι k**a**paree pickled capers

καπνιστό kapneest**o** smoked

καπουτσίνο kapoots**ee**no cappucino

καράφα kar**a**fa carafe

καρότο kar**o**to carrot

καρπούζι karp**oo**zee watermelon

καρύδι kar**ee**dhee walnut

καρυδόπιτα kareedh**o**peeta walnut cake

κασέρι kas**e**ree type of cheese

κάστανα k**a**stana chestnuts

καταΐφι kata**ee**fee small shredded pastry drenched in syrup

κατάλογος kat**a**loghos menu

κατάλογος κρασιών kat**a**loghos krasy**o**n wine list

καταψυγμένο katapseeghm**e**no frozen

κατσίκι kats**ee**kee roast kid

καφενείο kafen**ee**o café

καφές kaf**e**s coffee (Greek-style)

καφέδες kaf**e**dhes coffees (plural)

καφές γλυκύς kaf**e**s ghleek**ee**s very sweet coffee

καφές μέτριος kaf**e**s m**e**treeos medium-sweet coffee

καφές σκέτος kaf**e**s sk**e**tos coffee without sugar

κεράσια ker**a**sya cherries

κεφαλοτύρι kefalot**ee**ree type of cheese, often served fried in olive oil

κεφτέδες keft**e**dhes meat balls

κιμάς keem**a**s mince

κλέφτικο kl**e**fteeko casserole with lamb, potatoes and vegetables

κοκορέτσι kokor**e**tsee traditional spit-roasted dish of spiced liver and other offal

κολοκυθάκια kolokeeth**a**kya courgettes, zucchini

κολοκυθόπιτα kolokeeth**o**peeta courgette/zucchini pie

κονιάκ kony**a**k brandy, cognac

κοντοσούβλι kontos**oo**vlee spicy pieces of lamb, pork or beef, spit-roasted

κοτόπουλο kot**o**poolo chicken

κουλούρια kool**oo**rya bread rings

κουνέλι koon**e**lee rabbit

κουνουπίδι koonoop**ee**dhee cauliflower

κουπέπια koop**e**pya stuffed vine leaves (Cyprus)

κουπές koop**e**s meat pasties

κουραμπιέδες kooramby**e**dhes small almond cakes eaten at Christmas

κρασί kras**ee** wine

κρέας kr**e**as meat

κρέμα kr**e**ma cream

κρεμμύδια krem**ee**dhya onions

κρητική σαλάτα kreeteek**ee** sal**a**ta watercress salad

κρύο kr**ee**o cold

κυνήγι keen**ee**ghee game

κύριο πιάτο k**ee**reeo py**a**to main course

λ Λ

λαγός lagh**o**s hare

λάδι l**a**dhee oil

λαδότυρο ladh**o**teero soft cheese with olive oil

λάχανα l**a**khana green vegetables

λαχανικά lakhaneek**a** vegetables (menu heading)

λάχανο l**a**khano cabbage, greens

λεμονάδα lemon**a**dha lemon drink

λεμόνι lem**o**nee lemon

λευκό lefk**o** white (used for wine as well as **άσπρο**)

λίγο l**ee**gho a little, a bit

λουκάνικα look**a**neeka type of highly seasoned sausage

λουκουμάδες lookoom**a**dhes small fried dough balls in syrup

λουκούμι look**oo**mee Turkish delight

λούντζα l**oo**ndza loin of pork, marinated and smoked

μ Μ

μαγειρίτσα mayeer**ee**tsa soup made of lamb offal, special Easter dish

μαϊντανός maeedan**o**s parsley

μακαρόνια makar**o**nya spaghetti

μακαρόνια με κιμά makar**o**nya me keem**a** spaghetti bolognese

μαρίδες mar**ee**dhes small fish like sprats, served fried

μαρούλι mar**oo**lee lettuce

μαύρο κρασί m**a**vro kras**ee** red wine (although you'll hear k**o**keeno kras**ee** more often)

μανιτάρια maneet**a**rya mushrooms

μαυρομάτικα mavrom**a**teeka black-eyed peas

μεγάλο megh**a**lo large, big

μεζές mez**e**s (plural **μεζέδες** mez**e**dhes) small snacks served free of charge with ouzo or retsina; assortment of mini-portions of various dishes, available on the menu (or on request) at some restaurants

μεζεδοπωλείο mezedhopol**ee**o taverna/shop selling **mezedhes**

μέλι m**e**lee honey

μελιτζάνα meleetz**a**na aubergine (eggplant)

μελιτζάνες ιμάμ meleetz**a**nes eem**a**m aubergines (eggplants) stuffed with tomato and onion

μελιτζανοσαλάτα meleetzanos**a**lata aubergine (eggplant) mousse (dip)

μεσημεριανό meseemeryan**o** lunch

μεταλλικό νερό metaleek**o** ner**o** mineral water

μεταξά metaks**a** Metaxa (Greek brandy-type spirit)

μέτρια ψημένο metreea pseemeno medium-grilled (meat)

μη αεριούχο mee aereeookho still, not fizzy

μήλα meela apples

μηλόπιτα meelopeeta apple pie

μοσχάρι moskharee beef

μοσχάρι κοκινιστό moskharee kokeeneesto beef in wine sauce with tomatoes and onions

μουσακάς moosakas moussaka, layers of aubergine (eggplant), minced meat and potato, with white sauce

μπακαλιάρος bakalyaros cod

μπακαλιάρος παστός bakalyaros pastos salt cod

μπακλαβάς baklavas filo-pastry with nuts soaked in syrup

μπάμιες bamyes okra, ladies' fingers (vegetable)

μπαρμπούνι barboonee red mullet

μπέικον be-eekon bacon

μπιφτέκι beeftekee beef rissole/burger

μπουγάτσα booghatsa cheese or custard pastry sprinkled with sugar and cinnamon

μπουρέκι boorekee cheese, potato and courgette pie

μπουρέκια boorekya puff pastry filled with meat and cheese (Cyprus)

μπριάμ(ι) breeam(ee) ratatouille

μπριζόλα breezola steak/chop

μπριζόλα αρνίσια breezola arneesya lamb chop

μπριζόλα μοσχαρίσια breezola moskhareesya beef steak/chop

μπριζόλα χοιρινή breezola kheereenee pork chop
μπύρα beera beer
μύδια meedhya mussels

ν N

νες, νεσκαφέ nes, nescafe instant coffee (of any
  brand)
  νες με γάλα nes me ghala coffee (instant) with milk
  νες φραπέ nes frappe iced coffee
νερό nero water
ντολμάδες dolmadhes vine leaves, rolled up and
  stuffed with rice and sometimes mince
ντομάτες domates tomatoes
  ντομάτες γεμιστές domates yemeestes tomatoes
  stuffed with rice and herbs, and sometimes with
  mince

ξ Ξ

ξιφίας kseefeeas swordfish
ξύδι kseedhee vinegar

ο Ο

ομελέτα omeletta omelette
ορεκτικά orekteeka first courses/starters (menu
  heading)
ουζερί oozeree small bar selling ouzo and other
  drinks, maybe with **mezedhes** (**μεζέδες**)
ούζο oozo ouzo (traditional aniseed-flavoured spirit)
οχταπόδι okhtapodhee octopus (see also **χταπόδι**)

οχταπόδι κρασάτο okhtap**o**dhee krasato octopus in red wine sauce

π Π

παγάκια pagh**a**kya ice-cubes

παγωτό paghot**o** ice-cream

παϊδάκια paeedh**a**kya grilled lamb chops

παντζάρια pandz**a**rya beetroot with seasonings

παξιμάδια pakseem**a**dhya crispy bread (baked twice)

παπουτσάκια papoots**a**kya stuffed aubergines (eggplants)

πάστα p**a**sta cake, pastry

παστό past**o** salted

παστιτσάδα pasteets**a**da beef with tomatoes, onions, red wine, herbs, spices and pasta

παστίτσιο past**ee**tseeo baked pasta dish with a middle layer of meat and white sauce

πατσάς pats**a**s tripe soup

πατάτες pat**a**tes potatoes

πατάτες τηγανιτές pat**a**tes teeghaneet**e**s chips, fries

πεπόνι pep**o**nee melon

πιάτο της ημέρας p**ya**to tees eem**e**ras dish of the day

πιλάφι peel**a**fee rice

πιπέρι peep**e**ree pepper

πιπεριές peeper**ye**s peppers

πιπεριές γεμιστές peeper**ye**s yemeest**e**s stuffed peppers with rice, herbs and sometimes mince

141

πίτα or πίττα p**ee**ta pitta (flat unleavened bread); pie with different fillings, such as meat, cheese, vegetables

πλακί plak**ee** fish in tomato sauce

πορτοκαλάδα portokal**a**dha orangeade

πορτοκάλια portok**a**lya oranges

πουργούρι poorgh**oo**ree cracked wheat (Cyprus)

πουργούρι πιλάφι poorgh**oo**ree peel**a**fee salad made of cracked wheat (Cyprus)

πρωινό proeen**o** breakfast

ρ P

ραβιόλι ravy**o**lee pastry stuffed with cheese (Cyprus)

ραδίκια radh**ee**kya chicory

ρακή, ρακί rak**ee** raki, strong spirit a bit like schnapps

ρεβίθια rev**ee**thya chickpeas

ρέγγα r**e**nga herring

ρέγγα καπνιστή r**e**nga kapneest**ee** smoked herring, kipper

ρετσίνα rets**ee**na retsina, traditional resinated white wine

ρίγανη r**ee**ghanee oregano

ροδάκινο rodh**a**keeno peach

ροζέ κρασί roz**e** kras**ee** rosé wine

ρύζι r**ee**zee rice

ρυζόγαλο reez**o**ghalo rice pudding

σ ς Σ

σαγανάκι saghan**a**kee cheese coated in flour and fried in olive oil

σαλάτα sal**a**ta salad

σαλιγκάρια saleeng**a**rya snails

σαρδέλλες sardh**e**les sardines

σέλινο s**e**leeno celery, celeriac

σεφταλιά seftaly**a** minced pork pasty

σικαλένιο ψωμί seekal**e**nyo psom**ee** rye bread

σικώτι seek**o**tee liver

σκορδαλιά skordhaly**a** garlic and potato mash

σκορδαλιά με ψάρι τηγανιτό skordhaly**a** me ps**a**ree teeghaneet**o** fried fish served with garlic and potato mash

σκόρδο sk**o**rdho garlic

σόδα s**o**dha soda

σουβλάκι soovl**a**kee meat kebab

σουβλατζίδικο soovlats**ee**deeko shop selling souvlakia, doner kebabs, etc

σούπα s**oo**pa soup

σουπιά soopy**a** cuttlefish

σουτζουκάκια sootzook**a**kya highly seasoned meat balls

σπανάκι span**a**kee spinach

σπανακόπιτα spanak**o**peeta spinach pie

σπαράγγια σαλάτα spar**a**ngya sal**a**ta asparagus salad

σταφύλια staf**ee**lya grapes

στη σούβλα stee s**oo**vla spit-roasted

στιφάδο steef**a**dho braised beef in spicy onion and tomato sauce

στο φούρνο sto f**oo**rno baked in the oven

στρείδια str**ee**dhya oysters

σύκα s**ee**ka figs

σχάρας skh**a**ras grilled

τ T

ταραμοσαλάτα taramosal**a**ta mousse of cod roe

τζατζίκι tzatz**ee**kee yoghurt, garlic and cucumber dip

τηγανιτό teeghaneet**o** fried

τραπανός trapan**os** soup made of cracked wheat and yoghurt (Cyprus)

τραπέζι trap**e**zee table

τσάι ts**a**ee tea

τσιπούρα tseep**oo**ra type of sea bream

τσουρέκι tsoor**e**kee festive bread

τυρί teer**ee** cheese

τυροκαυτερή teerokafter**ee** spicy dip made of cheese and peppers

τυρόπιτα teer**o**peeta cheese pie

τυροσαλάτα teerosal**a**ta starter made of cream cheese and herbs

φ Φ

φάβα f**a**va yellow split peas or lentils, served in a purée with olive oil and capers

φακές fak**es** lentils

φασολάδα fasol**a**dha soup made with white beans and vegetables, eaten with lemon

φασολάκια fasol**a**kya green beans

φασόλια fas**o**lya haricot beans

φέτα f**e**ta feta cheese, tangy white cheese used in salads and other dishes; a slice

φλαούνες fla**oo**nes Easter cheese cake (Cyprus)

φράουλες fr**a**ooles strawberries

φραπέ frapp**e** iced coffee

φρέσκο fr**e**sko fresh

φυστίκια Αιγίνης feest**ee**kya egh**ee**nees pistacchios

χ X

χαλβάς khalv**a**s sesame seed sweet

χαλούμι khal**oo**mee ewe's- or goat's-milk cheese, often grilled

χοιρινό kheereen**o** pork

χόρτα kh**o**rta wild greens (similar to spinach) eaten cold with oil and lemon

χορτοφάγος khortof**a**ghos vegetarian

χούμους kh**oo**moos dip made with puréed chickpeas, hummus (Cyprus)

χταπόδι khtap**o**dhee octopus, grilled or as a side-salad

χωριάτικη σαλάτα khory**a**teekee sal**a**ta salad, Greek-style, with tomatoes, feta cheese, cucumber, onions, olives and oregano

ψ æ

ψάρι psaree fish

ψάρια καπνιστά psarya kapneesta smoked fish

ψάρια πλακί psarya plakee baked whole fish with
  vegetables and tomatoes

ψαρόσουπα psarosoopa seafood soup

ψαροταβέρνα psarotaverna fish taverna

ψησταριά pseestarya grill house

ψητό pseeto roast/grilled

ψωμί psomee bread

ψωμί ολικής αλέσεως psomee oleekees aleseos
  wholemeal bread

Phonetic menu reader

••••••••••••••••••••••••••••••••••

aeree**oo**kho fizzy, sparkling

af**e**leea pork in red wine with seasonings (Cyprus)

aghreeogh**oo**roono wild boar

akheen**ee** sea urchin roes

akhl**a**dhee pear

akhl**a**dhee sto f**oo**rno baked pear in syrup sauce

akhneest**o** steamed

al**a**tee salt

al**e**vree flour

alevr**o**peeta pie made with cheese, milk and eggs

am**ee**ghdhala almonds

aneethos dill

ang**oo**ree cucumber

ankeen**a**res **a**la pol**ee**ta artichokes with lemon juice and olive oil

ankeen**a**res artichokes

arak**a**s peas

arn**ee** lamb

arn**ee** lemon**a**to lamb braised in sauce with herbs and lemon juice

arn**ee** me v**o**tana lamb braised with vegetables and herbs

arn**ee** pseet**o** roast lamb

arn**ee** yoov**e**tsee roast lamb with small pasta

arn**ee**see-es breez**o**les lamb chops

aspro kras**ee** white wine

aspro white

astak**o**s lobster (often served with lemon juice and olive oil)

ather**ee**na whitebait, usually fried

avgh**a** eggs

avghol**e**mono egg and lemon soup

avghot**a**rakho mullet roe (smoked)

bakalee**a**ros cod

bakalee**a**ros past**o**s salt cod

baklav**a**s filo-pastry with nuts soaked in syrup

b**a**meeyes okra, ladies' fingers (vegetable)

bar**a**kee bar

barb**oo**nee red mullet

be-**ee**kon bacon

beeft**e**kee beef rissole/burger

b**ee**ra beer

boogh**a**tsa cheese or custard pastry sprinkled with sugar and cinnamon

book**a**lee bottle

boordh**e**to fish or meat in a thick sauce of onions, tomatoes and red peppers

boor**e**kee cheese potato, and courgette pie

boor**e**keea puff pastry filled with meat and cheese (Cyprus)

bree**a**m(ee) ratatouille

breez**o**la steak/chop

breez**o**la arn**ee**sya lamb chop

breez**o**la kheereen**ee** pork chop
breez**o**la moskhar**ee**sya beef steak/chop

dendrol**ee**vano rosemary
dh**a**fnee bay leaf
dh**a**kteela almond cakes
dham**a**skeena plums, prunes
dh**ee**ples pastry with honey and walnuts
dh**ee**pno dinner
dholm**a**dhes vine leaves, rolled up and stuffed with
    minced meat and rice
dolm**a**dhes vine leaves, rolled up and stuffed with rice
    and sometimes mince
dom**a**tes tomatoes
dom**a**tes yemeest**e**s tomatoes stuffed with rice and
    herbs, and sometimes with mince

eem**a**m baeeld**ee** stuffed aubergines (eggplants)
eenopol**ee**o wine shop
eksokheek**o** stuffed pork or beef with vegetables
    and cheese
el**a**kheesta pseem**e**no rare (meat)
ele**o**ladho olive oil
el**y**es olives
el**y**es tsakeest**e**s cracked green olives with coriander
    seeds and garlic (Cyprus)
elyot**ee** olive bread
esteeat**o**reeo restaurant

fak**es** lentils

fangr**ee** sea bream

fasol**a**dha soup made with white beans and
  vegetables, eaten with lemon

fasol**a**keea green beans

fas**o**leea haricot beans

f**a**va yellow split peas or lentils, served in a purée
  with olive oil and capers

feest**ee**kya peanuts

feest**ee**kya egh**ee**nees pistacchios

f**e**ta feta cheese, tangy white cheese used in salads
  and other dishes; a slice

fla**oo**nes Easter cheese cake (Cyprus)

fra**oo**les strawberries

frapp**e** iced coffee

fr**e**sko fresh

g**a**vros sardine-type fish (if salted: anchovy)

gh**a**la milk

ghalaktob**oo**reeko custard tart

ghalaktopol**ee**o café/patisserie

ghar**ee**dhes shrimps; prawns

ghar**ee**dhes yoov**e**tsee prawns in tomato sauce
  with feta

ghar**ee**falo clove (spice)

ghaz**o**za fizzy drink

ghleek**a** desserts

ghleek**a** kootaly**oo** crystallized fruits in syrup

ghl**o**sa sole
gh**o**pes bogue, a type of fish
ghravy**e**ra cheese resembling gruyère
kaf**e**dhes coffees (plural)
kafen**ee**o café
kaf**e**s coffee (Greek-style)
kaf**e**s ghleek**ee**s very sweet coffee
kaf**e**s m**e**treeos medium-sweet coffee
kaf**e**s sk**e**tos coffee without sugar
kakav**ee**a fish soup
kak**o**w hot chocolate
kalam**a**kee straw (for drinking); small skewer
kalam**a**reea squid
kalam**a**reea teeghaneet**a** fried squid
kalamb**o**kee corn on the cob
kalambok**o**peeta corn bread
kalopseem**e**no well done (meat)
kan**e**lla cinnamon
k**a**paree pickled capers
kapneest**o** smoked
kapoots**ee**no cappucino
kar**a**fa carafe
karav**ee**dha crayfish
kar**ee**dha coconut
kar**ee**dhee walnut
kareedh**o**peeta walnut cake
kar**e**kla chair
kar**o**to carrot

karp**oo**zee watermelon
kas**e**ree type of cheese
ka**s**tana chestnuts
kata**ee**fee small shredded pastry drenched in syrup
kat**a**loghos menu
kat**a**loghos krasy**o**n wine list
katapseeghm**e**no frozen
kats**ee**kee roast kid
ka**v**a wine shop
ka**v**ooras boiled crab
kayan**a**s me past**o** kr**e**yas salted pork with cheese, tomatoes and eggs
keedh**o**nee quince
keedh**o**nee sto f**oo**rno baked quince
keedh**o**neea type of clams, cockles
keem**a**s mince
keen**ee**ghee game
k**ee**reeo pya**t**o main course
kefalot**ee**ree type of cheese, often served fried in olive oil
keft**e**dhes meat balls
ker**a**seea cherries
khal**oo**mee ewe's- or goat's-milk cheese, often grilled
khalv**a**s sesame seed sweet
kheere**e**no pork
kheere**e**no kreete**e**ko baked pork chops (Crete)
kheerom**e**ree marinated, smoked ham
kh**e**lee kapneest**o** smoked eel

kh**oo**moos dip made with puréed chickpeas, hummus (Cyprus)

khoree**a**teekee sal**a**ta salad, Greek-style, with tomatoes, feta cheese, cucumber, onions, olives and oregano

kh**o**rta wild greens (similar to spinich) eaten cold with oil and lemon

khortof**a**ghos vegetarian

khtap**o**dhee octopus, grilled or as a side-salad

kl**e**fteeko casserole with lamb, potatoes and vegetables

kokor**e**tsee traditional spit-roasted dish of spiced liver and other offal

kokt**e-ee**l cocktail

kolatsy**o** brunch, elevenses

kolokeeth**a**keea courgettes, zucchini

kolokeeth**o**peeta courgette/zucchini pie

kolokeeth**o**peeta gleeky**a** sweet courgette/ zucchini pie

kolok**o**tes pastries with pumpkin seeds and raisins

kontos**oo**vlee spicy pieces of lamb, pork or beef, spit-roasted

kony**a**k brandy, cognac

kooky**a** broad beans

kool**oo**reea bread rings

koon**e**lee rabbit

koonoop**ee**dhee cauliflower

koop**e**peea stuffed vine leaves (Cyprus)

153

koopes meat pasties

koorambyedhes small almond cakes eaten at
  Christmas

kotopoolo chicken

kotopoolo kapama chicken casseroled with red
  peppers, onions, cinnamon and raisins

kotopoolo reeghanato grilled basted chicken
  with herbs

krasee wine

kreas meat

kreeo cold

kreeteekee salata watercress salad

krema cream

kremeedheea onions

kseedhee vinegar

kseefeeas swordfish

ladhee oil

ladhera vegetable casserole

ladhoteero soft cheese with olive oil

laghos hare

lakhana green vegetables

lakhaneeka vegetables (menu heading)

lakhano cabbage, greens

lavrakee sea-bass

leegho a little, a bit

lefko white

lemonadha lemon drink

lem**o**nee lemon
look**a**neeka type of highly seasoned sausage
look**oo**m**a**dhes small fried dough balls in syrup
look**oo**mee Turkish delight
look**oo**meea shortbread served at weddings
l**oo**ndza loin of pork, marinated and smoked

maeedan**o**s parsley
makar**o**nya spaghetti
makar**o**nya me keem**a** spaghetti bolognese
maneet**a**reea mushrooms
mar**ee**dhes small fish like sprats, served fried
mar**oo**lee lettuce
mart**ee**nee martini
m**a**vro kras**ee** red wine (although you'll hear kokeeno
   kras**ee** more often)
mavrom**a**teeka black-eyed peas
mayeer**ee**tsa soup made of lamb offal, special
   Easter dish
mee aeree**oo**kho still, not fizzy
m**ee**dheea mussels
meekr**o** small, little
m**ee**la apples
m**ee**lko chocolate milk
meelks**e**ik milkshake
meel**o**peeta apple pie
megh**a**lo large, big
m**e**lee honey

meleetz**a**na aubergine (eggplant)

meleetzan**a**kee gleek**o** crystallized sweet in syrup, made from aubergine/eggplant

meleetz**a**nes eem**a**m aubergines (eggplants) stuffed with tomato and onion

meleetzanosal**a**ta aubergine (eggplant) mousse (dip)

meseemeree**a**n**o** lunch

metaks**a** Metaxa (Greek brandy-type spirit)

metaleek**o** ner**o** mineral water

m**e**treea pseem**e**no medium-grilled (meat)

mezedhopol**ee**o taverna/shop selling mezedhes

mez**e**s (plural **μεζέδες** mez**e**dhes) small snacks served free of charge with ouzo or retsina; assortment of mini-portions of various dishes, available on the menu (or on request) at some restaurants.

moosak**a**s moussaka, layers of aubergine (eggplant), minced meat and potato, with white sauce

moskh**a**ree beef

moskh**a**ree kokeeneest**o** beef in wine sauce with tomatoes and onions

ner**o** water

nes frapp**e** iced coffee

nes me gh**a**la coffee (instant) with milk

nes, nescaf**e** instant coffee (of any brand)

okhtap**o**dhee octopus (see also **χταπόδι**)

okhtap**o**dhee kras**a**to octopus in red wine sauce

omel**e**tta omelette

oozeree small bar selling ouzo
   and other drinks, maybe with mezedhes

oozo ouzo (traditional aniseed-flavoured spirit)

orekteek**a** first courses/starters (menu heading)

oveleest**ee**reeo shop selling souvlakia and doner
   kebabs

paeedh**a**keea grilled lamb chops

pagh**a**kya ice-cubes

paghot**o** ice-cream

pakseem**a**dheea crispy bread (baked twice)

pakseemadhok**oo**loora tomato and cheese bread

pandz**a**reea beetroot with seasonings

papoots**a**keea stuffed aubergines (eggplants)

pasat**e**mpo pumpkin seeds

p**a**sta cake, pastry

pasteets**a**da beef with tomatoes, onions, red wine,
   herbs, spices and pasta

past**ee**tseeo baked pasta dish with a middle layer of
   meat and white sauce

past**o** salted

pat**a**tes potatoes

pat**a**tes teeghaneet**e**s chips, fries

pats**a**s tripe soup

peek**a**nteeko spicy

peel**a**fee rice

peeleeor**ee**teeko boob**a**ree spicy sausage

peep**e**ree pepper

peep**e**ry**e**s peppers

peep**e**ry**e**s yemeest**e**s stuffed peppers with rice, herbs and sometimes mince

p**ee**ta pitta (flat unleavened bread); pie with different fillings, such as meat, cheese, vegetables

pep**o**nee melon

p**e**strofa trout

plak**ee** fish in tomato sauce

poorgh**oo**ree cracked wheat (Cyprus)

poorgh**oo**ree peel**a**fee salad made of cracked wheat (Cyprus)

portokal**a**dha orangeade

portok**a**lya oranges

pr**a**sa me sees**a**mee leeks baked and sprinkled with sesame seeds

proeen**o** breakfast

ps**a**ree fish

ps**a**reea kapneest**a** smoked fish

ps**a**reea plak**ee** baked whole fish with vegetables and tomatoes

psar**o**soopa seafood soup

psarotav**e**rna fish taverna

pseestaree**a** grill house

pseet**o** roast/grilled

psom**a**kee bread roll, bread bun

psom**ee** bread

psom**ee** oleek**ee**s al**e**seos wholemeal bread

py**a**to tees eem**e**ras dish of the day

radh**ee**keea chicory

rak**ee** raki, strong spirit a bit like schnapps

ravee**o**lee pastry stuffed with cheese (Cyprus)

r**ee**ghanee oregano

r**ee**zee rice

reez**o**ghalo rice pudding

r**e**nga herring

r**e**nga kapneest**ee** smoked herring, kipper

rets**ee**na retsina, traditional resinated white wine

rev**ee**theea chickpeas

rodh**a**keeno peach

rol**o** me keem**a** meatloaf

r**o**seekee sal**a**ta Russian salad (pieces of egg, potatoes, gherkins, peas and carrots in mayonnaise)

roz**e** kras**ee** rosé wine

saghan**a**kee cheese coated in flour and fried in olive oil

sal**a**khee ray

sal**a**ta salad

salat**ee**k**a** salads (menu heading)

saleeng**a**reea snails

saleeng**a**reea yakhn**ee** snails in tomato sauce

s**a**ndweets sandwich (sometimes a filled roll, sometimes a toasted sandwich with your own chosen combination of fillings)

saranghl**ee** pastry with walnuts, sesame seeds and syrup; sometimes chocolate too

sardh**e**les sardines

s**ee**ka figs

s**ee**ka sto f**oo**rno me mavrod**a**fnee figs cooked in red wine sauce with spices

seekal**e**nyo psom**ee** rye bread

seek**o**tee liver

seftaly**a** minced pork pasty

s**e**leeno celery, celeriac

skh**a**ras grilled

skordhaly**a** garlic and potato mash

skordhaly**a** me ps**a**ree teeghaneet**o** fried fish served with garlic and potato mash

sk**o**rdho garlic

s**o**dha soda

sofr**ee**to beef stew with creamy garlic sauce (Corfu)

s**oo**pa soup

soopy**a** cuttlefish

sootzook**a**kya highly seasoned meat balls

soovl**a**kee meat kebab

soovlats**ee**deeko shop selling souvlakia, doner kebabs, etc

span**a**kee spinach

spanak**o**peeta spinach pie

spar**a**ngee asparagus

spar**a**ngya ke angeen**a**res asparagus and artichokes with lemon

spar**a**ngya sal**a**ta asparagus salad

staf**ee**lya grapes

stee s**oo**vla spit-roasted

steef**a**dho braised beef in spicy onion and tomato sauce

sto f**oo**rno baked in the oven

str**ee**dhya oysters

takh**ee**nee sesame seed paste

taramosal**a**ta mousse of cod roe

teeghaneet**o** fried

teer**ee** cheese

teerokafter**ee** spicy dip made of cheese and peppers

teer**o**peeta cheese pie

teerosal**a**ta starter made of cream cheese and herbs

thalaseen**a** seafood

theem**a**ree thyme

t**o**nos pseet**o**s grilled tuna with vegetables

trapan**o**s soup made of cracked wheat and yoghurt (Cyprus)

trap**e**zee table

ts**a**ee tea

tseep**oo**ra type of sea bream

tsoor**e**kee festive bread

tzatz**ee**kee yoghurt, garlic and cucumber dip

vaseeleek**o**s basil

veeseen**o** kas**e**ree sheep's cheese served with cherry preserve

ver**ee**koko apricot

vl**ee**ta wild greens (like spinach, eaten with olive oil and lemon)

vodheen**o** beef
voot**ee**mata biscuits to dip in coffee
v**oo**teero butter
v**o**tka vodka
vradeen**o** evening meal
vrast**o** boiled

weeskee whisky
yakhn**ee** cooked in tomato sauce and olive oil
ya**oo**rtee yoghurt
ya**oo**rtee me m**e**lee yoghurt with honey
y**ee**da vrast**ee** goat soup
y**ee**ghantes large butter beans
y**ee**ros doner kebab
yemeest**a** stuffed vegetables
yoovarl**a**kya meatballs in lemon sauce

z**a**kharee sugar
zakharoplast**ee**o cake shop
zamb**o**n ham
zelat**ee**na brawn
zest**ee** sokol**a**ta hot chocolate
zest**o** hot, warm

Grammar

The following basic rules of Greek grammar will help you make full use of the information in this book. Greek grammar is rather complicated by the fact that pronouns, nouns and adjectives change their endings according to their function in the sentence, their number (whether they are singular or plural) and their gender (whether they are masculine, feminine or neuter) – rather like German. A brief outline of the grammar is given here, but for a fuller explanation you should consult a Greek grammar book.

Nouns

••

A noun is a word used to refer to a person or thing, e.g. 'car', 'horse', 'Mary'. Greek nouns can be masculine, feminine or neuter, and the words for 'the' and 'a' (the articles) change according to the gender of the noun.

o (o)	= the with masculine nouns
η (ee)	= the with feminine nouns

το (to)	= the with neuter nouns
ένας (**e**nas)	= a with masculine nouns
μία (m**ee**a)	= a with feminine nouns
ένα (**e**na)	= a with neuter nouns

The article is the most reliable indication of the gender of a noun, i.e. whether it is masculine, feminine or neuter.

In the dictionary sections you will come across examples like this: **ο/η γιατρός** (yatr**o**s) doctor. This means that the same ending is used for men as well as women doctors i.e. **ο γιατρός** is a male doctor, **η γιατρός** is a female doctor.

You will also encounter entries like **ο Άγγλος/η Αγγλίδα** indicating that an Englishman is referred to as **ο Άγγλος** (**a**nglos) while an Englishwoman is **η Αγγλίδα** (angl**ee**dha).

Masculine endings of nouns

The most common endings of masculine nouns are **–ος** (os), **–ας** (as), **–ης** (ees), e.g.

ο καιρός (ker**o**s)	weather
ο πατέρας (pat**e**ras)	father
ο κυβερνήτης (keevern**ee**tees)	captain
	(of aeroplane)

Feminine endings of nouns

The most common endings of feminine nouns are
–α (a), **–η** (ee), e.g.

η μητέρα (meet**e**ra)	mother
η Κρήτη (kr**ee**tee)	Crete

Neuter endings of nouns

The most common neuter endings are: **–o** (o), **–ι** (ee),
e.g.

το κτίριο (kt**ee**reeo)	building
το πορτοκάλι (portok**a**lee)	orange (fruit)

Plurals

The article 'the' changes in the plural. For masculine
(**o**) and feminine (**η**) nouns it becomes **οι** (ee).
For neuter nouns (**το**) it becomes **τα** (ta).

Nouns have different endings in the plural.
Masculine nouns change their endings to **–οι** (ee),
e.g.

ο βράχος (vr**a**khos)	οι βράχοι (vr**a**khee)

Feminine nouns change their endings to **–ες** (es), e.g.

η κυρία (ker**ee**a)	οι κυρίες (ker**ee**-es)

Neuter nouns change their endings to –**α** (a), e.g.

το κτίριο (kt**ee**reeo)   **τα κτίρια** (kt**ee**reea)

There are many exceptions to the above rules, such as:

ο άντρας (**a**ndhras)   **οι άντρες** (**a**ndhres)

Adjectives

An adjective is a word that describes or gives extra information about a person or thing, e.g. 'small', 'pretty' or 'practical'. Greek adjectives have endings that change according to the gender and number of the noun they describe, e.g.

ο καλός πατέρας (kal**o**s pat**e**ras)	the good father
η καλή κυρία (kal**ee** ker**ee**a)	the good lady
οι καλοί πατέρες (kal**ee** pat**e**res)	the good fathers
οι καλές κυρίες (kal**e**s ker**ee**-es)	the good ladies

In the Greek–English dictionary section of this book, all adjectives are given with their endings clearly shown, e.g.

κρύος/α/ο (kr**ee**-os/a/o)   cold

166

By far the most common adjective endings are **−ος** (os) for masculine, **−α** (a) for feminine and **−ο** (o) for neuter nouns.

Possessive adjectives

••••••••••••••••••••••••••••••••••

In Greek, adjectives go before the noun they describe, but the possessive adjectives (my, your, his, etc.) follow the noun. They don't change according to the gender and number of the noun. The article is still added in front of the noun.

my	**μου**	moo
your	**σου**	soo
his	**του**	too
her	**της**	tees
its	**του**	too
our	**μας**	mas
your (plural) (This is also the polite form)	**σας**	sas
their	**τους**	toos

my key   **το κλειδί μου** (to kleeth**ee** moo)
your room   **το δωμάτιό σας** (to dhom**a**tee**o** sas)

Verbs

•••

A verb is a word used to say what someone or something does or what happens, e.g. 'sing', 'walk', 'rain'. Unlike verbs in English, Greek verbs have a different ending for each person, singular and plural. The most essential verbs in Greek are the verbs **είμαι** 'I am' and **έχω** 'I have'.

to be

είμαι	I am	**ee**me
είσαι	you are	**ee**se
είναι	he/she/it is	**ee**ne
είμαστε	we are	**ee**maste
είστε	you are	**ee**ste*
είναι	they are	**ee**ne

* This form is also used when addressing someone you do not know very well; it is generally referred to as the polite plural (like the French 'vous').

Note: While in English it is necessary to use the personal pronoun, i.e. we, you etc, in order to distinguish between 'we are', 'you are' etc, in Greek this function is carried out by the different endings of the verb itself. Thus, in Greek, 'we are' and 'they are' can be simply **είμαστε** (**ee**maste), **είναι** (**ee**ne).

to have

έχω	I have	**e**kho
έχεις	you have	**e**khees
έχει	he/she/it has	**e**khee
έχουμε	we have	**e**khoome
έχετε	you have	**e**khete
έχουν	they have	**e**khoon

Note: As above, 'I have' can be expressed in Greek with simply the verb έχω; each ending is particular to a specific person.

Verbs in Greek, in the active voice, end in –ω (o) or –ώ (o). This is the ending with which they generally appear in dictionaries. Note that in everyday speech a more usual ending for –ώ (o) is –άω (ao). If a verb does not have an active voice form, in a dictionary it will appear with the ending –μαι (-me), e.g.

λυπάμαι (leepame) to be sad or sorry
θυμάμαι (theemame) to remember

The verb αγαπώ (aghapo) 'to love' has typical endings for verbs ending in –ώ (-o), while those ending in –ω (-o) follow the pattern of έχω (**e**kho) above.

αγαπώ/άω (aghap**o**/a**o**)	I love
αγαπάς (aghap**as**)	you love
αγαπά (aghap**a**)	he/she/it loves

αγαπούμε (aghap**oo**me)   we love
αγαπάτε (aghap**a**te)   you love
αγαπούν (aghap**oo**n)   they love

Negative

· ·

To make a sentence negative, you put **δεν** (dhen)
immediately before the verb, e.g.

I don't know   **δεν ξέρω**   dhen ks**e**ro
I have no...   **δεν έχω**...   dhen **e**kho

Future

· ·

The future tense is made by adding **θα** (tha)
immediately before the verb, e.g.

θα πάω tha pao   I shall go
δε θα πάω dhe tha p**a**o   I shall not go

Forms of address

●●●●●●●●●●●●●●●●●●●●●●●●●●●●●●●●●●●●●●●

In Greek, there are two ways of addressing people,
depending on their age, social or professional
status, and how formal or informal the relationship
is between two people. For example, an older
person will probably speak to a much younger one
using the singular (informal) but the younger
person will use the plural (formal) unless well
acquainted. Two friends will speak to each other
using the informal singular:

Τι κάνεις; (tee ka**nees**?)   How are you?
Καλά, εσύ; (kal**a** es**ee**?)   Fine, and you?

But two acquaintances will address each other in
a more formal way, using the plural:

Τι κάνετε; (tee ka**nete**?)   How are you?
Καλά, εσείς; (kal**a**, es**ees**?)   Fine, and you?

Personal pronouns

A pronoun is a word used to refer to someone or something that has been mentioned earlier, e.g. 'it', 'they', 'him'. There are times when a personal pronoun needs to be used in Greek, e.g. in order to establish the sex of the person or the gender of the thing referred to, i.e. he, she or it.

εγώ	I	egho
εσύ	you	esee
αυτός	he	aftos
αυτή	she	aftee
αυτό	it	afto
εμείς	we	emees
εσείς	you	esees
αυτοί	they (masculine)	aftee
αυτές	they (feminine)	aftes
αυτά	they (neuter)	afta

Thus:

αυτός έχει (aftos ekhee)   he has
αυτή έχει (aftee ekhee)   she has

Public holidays

•••••••••••••••••••••••••••••••••••••••

January 1	**Πρωτοχρονιά** New Year's Day
January 6	**Θεοφάνεια** Epiphany
Late February/ early March (40 days before Easter)	**Καθαρά Δευτέρα (Αρχή Σαρακοστής)** Ash Monday
March 25	**Ο Ευαγγελισμός/Εθνική γιορτή της Ανεξαρτησίας** Annunciation and Greek Independence Day
April/May (Good Friday to Easter Monday)	**Πάσχα** Easter
May 1	**Εργατική Ημέρα Πρωτομαγιάς** Labour Day
May/June	**Πεντηκοστή** Whit Monday
August 15	**Ανάληψη (της Παναγίας)** Assumption (of the Virgin Mary)
October 28	The "Ochi" Day: 2nd World War Memorial Day
December 25	**Χριστούγεννα** Christmas Day
December 26	**Δεύτερη Ημέρα των Χριστουγέννων** Boxing Day/St Stephen's Day

English – Greek

A

a (masculine o words)	ένας	enas
a (feminine η words)	μία	meea
(neuter το words)	ένα	ena
about: a book about Athens	ένα βιβλίο για την Αθήνα	ena veevleeo ya teen Atheena
at about ten o'clock	περίπου στις δέκα	pereepoo stees dheka
above	πάνω από	pano apo
accident	το ατύχημα	to ateekheema
accommodation	η κατάλυμα	to kataleema
address	η διεύθυνση	ee dheeeftheensee
admission charge	η είσοδος	ee eesodhos
adult	ο ενήλικος	o eneeleekos
advance: in advance	προκατα-βολικώς	prokatavoleekos
Aegean Sea	το Αιγαίο (πέλαγος)	to egheo (pelaghos)

after	μετά	meta
afternoon	το απόγευμα	to apoyevma
again	πάλι/ ξανά	palee/ ksana
ago: a week ago	πριν μια βδομάδα	preen mya vdhomadha
air conditioning	ο κλιματισμός	o kleemateesmos
airline	η αεροπορική εταιρία	ee aeroporeekee etereea
airplane	το αεροπλάνο	to aeroplano
airport	το αεροδρόμιο	to aerodhromeeo
airport bus	το λεωφορείο για/	to leoforeeo ya/
	το αεροδρό-μειο	to aerodhromeeo
air ticket	το αεροπορικό εισιτήριο	to aeroporeeko eeseeteereeo
alarm (emergency)	ο συναγερμός	o seenayermos
alarm clock	το ξυπνητήρι	to kseepneeteeree
alcohol	το αλκοόλ	to alko-ol

English	Greek	Pronunciation	English	Greek	Pronunciation
alcohol-free	χωρίς αλκοόλ	khorees alko-ol	to answer	απαντώ	apando
alcoholic	οινοπνευμα-τώδης	eenopnevma-todhees	answerphone	ο αυτόματος τηλεφωνητής	o aftomatos teelefoneetees
all	όλος	olos	antibiotics	τα αντιβιοτικά	ta andeeveeo-teeka
all the milk	όλο το γάλα	olo to ghala	antiseptic	το αντισηπτικό	to andeeseep-teeko
all the time	όλον τον καιρό	olon ton kero	apartment	το διαμέρισμα	to dheeamer-eesma
allergic to	αλλεργικός σε	alenyeekos se	arm	το μπράτσο	to bratso
all right (agreed)	εντάξει	endaksee	around	γύρω	yeero
also	επίσης	epeesees	arrivals	οι αφίξεις	ee afeeksees
always	πάντα	panda	to arrive	φτάνω	ftano
ambulance	το ασθενοφόρο	to asthenoforo	aspirin	η ασπιρίνη	ee aspeereenee
America	η Αμερική	ee amereekee	asthma	το άσθμα	to asthma
American	ο Αμερικανός/ η Αμερικανίδα	o amereekanos/ ee amereeka-needha	at	σε	se
and	και	ke	at the (masculine, neuter)	στο	sto
angry	θυμωμένος	theemomenos	at the (feminine)	στη	stee
another	άλλος	alos			
another beer	άλλη μια μπίρα	alee mea beera			
answer	η απάντηση	ee apandeesee			

English – Greek

English - Greek

English	Greek	Pronunciation
attractive (person)	ελκυστικός	elkeesteekos
Australia	η Αυστραλία	ee afstraleea
Australian	ο Αυστραλός/	o afstralos/
	η Αυστραλέζα	ee afstraleza
automatic	αυτόματος	aftomatos
autumn	το φθινόπωρο	to ftheenoporo
awful	φοβερός	foveros
B		
baby	το μωρό	to moro
baby's bottle	το μπιμπερό	to beebero
baby seat (in car)	το παιδικό	to pedheeko
	κάθισμα	katheesma
baby-sitter	η μπεϊμπισίτερ	ee babysitter
baby wipes	τα υγρά	ta eeghra
	μαντηλάκια	mandeelakya
	για μωρά	ya mora
back (of a person)	η πλάτη	ee platee

English	Greek	Pronunciation
bad (of food)	χαλασμένος	khalasmenos
bad (of weather)	κακός	kakos
bag (small)	η τσάντα	ee tsanda
(suitcase)	η βαλίτσα	ee valeetsa
baggage	οι αποσκευές	ee aposkeves
bank	η τράπεζα	ee trapeza
banknote	το χαρτονό-	to khartono-
	μισμα	meesma
bar	το μπαρ	to bar
bath (tub)	το μπάνιο	to banyo
to take a bath	κάνω μπάνιο	kano banyo
bathroom	το μπάνιο	to banyo
battery	η μπαταρία	ee bataree-a
beach	η πλαζ/	ee plaz/
	η παραλία	ee paraleea
beautiful	όμορφος	omorfos
because	επειδή	epeedee
bed	το κρεβάτι	to krevatee
double bed	διπλό κρεβάτι	dheeplo krevatee
single bed	μονό κρεβάτι	mono krevatee

twin beds	δύο μονά κρεβάτια	dheeo mona krevatya
bedroom	η κρεβατοκάμαρα	ee krevatokamara
beer	η μπύρα	ee beera
before (time)	πριν (από)	preen (apo)
(place)	μπροστά από	brosta apo
to begin	αρχίζω	arkheezo
behind	πίσω από	peeso apo
to believe	πιστεύω	peestevo
below	κάτω από	kato apo
beside	δίπλα	dheepla
best	ο καλύτερος	o kaleeteros
better (than)	καλύτερος (από)	kaleeteros (apo)
between	μεταξύ	metaksee
bicycle	το ποδήλατο	to podheelato
big	μεγάλος	meghalos
bigger	μεγαλύτερος	meghaleeteros
bill	ο λογαριασμός	o logharyasmos

birthday	τα γενέθλια	ta venethleea
happy birthday!	χρόνια πολλά	khronya pola
biscuit	το μπισκότο	to beeskoto
bit: a bit (of)	λίγο	leegho
bite (insect)	το τσίμπημα	to tseebeema
bitten: I have been bitten	με δάγκωσε	me dhangose
bitter	πικρός	peekros
black	μαύρος	mavros
blocked (pipe)	βουλωμένος	voolomenos
(nose)	κλειστή	kleestee
blood pressure	η πίεση αίματος	ee peeyesee ematos
blouse	η μπλούζα	ee blooza
blow-dry	στέγνωμα	steghnoma
blue	γαλάζιος/μπλε	ghalazyos/ble
boat (small)	η βάρκα	ee varka
(ship)	το πλοίο	to pleeo
to boil	βράζω	vrazo

book	η το βιβλίο	to veevleeo
to book	κλείνω	kleeno
(room, tickets)		
booking; to make a booking	κλείνω θέση	kleeno thesee
booking office (railways, airlines, etc.)	το εκδοτήριο	to ekdhoteereeo
(theatre)	το ταμείο	to tameeo
bookshop	το βιβλιοπωλείο	to veevleeopoleeo
boots	οι μπότες	ee botes
boring	βαρετός	varetos
bottle	το μπουκάλι	to bookalee
box office	το ταμείο	to tameeo
boy	το αγόρι	to aghoree
boyfriend	ο φίλος	o feelos
to brake	φρενάρω	frenaro
brakes	τα φρένα	ta frena

bread (wholemeal)	το ψωμί	to psomee
	ψωμί ολικής αλέσεως	psomee oleekees aleseos
to break	σπάζω	spazo
breakfast	το πρωινό	to proeeno
breast	το στήθος	to steethos
to breathe	αναπνέω	anapneo
bride	η νύφη	ee neefee
bridegroom	ο γαμπρός	o ghambros
to bring	φέρνω	ferno
Britain	η Βρετανία	ee vretaneea
British	ο Βρετανός/ η Βρετανίδα	o vretanos/ ee vretaneedha
broken	σπασμένος	spasmenos
broken down	χαλασμένος	khalasmenos
brother	ο αδελφός	o adhelfos
brown	καφέ	kafe
bulb (light)	ο γλόμπος	o ghlobos
bureau de change (bank)	ξένο συνάλλαγμα	kseno seenalaghma

English	Greek	Pronunciation
bus	το λεωφορείο	to leoforeeo
business	η δουλειά	ee dhoolya
business centre	το εμπορικό κέντρο	to emboreeko kendro
bus station	ο σταθμός του λεωφορείου	o stathmos too leoforeeoo
bus stop	η στάση του λεωφορείου	ee stasee too leoforeeoo
bus terminal	το τέρμα του λεωφορείου	to terma too leoforeeoo
busy	απασχολη–μένος	apaskholeemenos
but	αλλά	ala
to buy	αγοράζω	aghorazo
C		
cab	το ταξί	to taksee
café	το καφενείο	to kafeneeo
cake	το γλύκισμα	o ghleekeesma
to call	φωνάζω	fonazo
call (telephone)	η κλήση	ee kleesee
long-distance call	η υπεραστική κλήση	ee eeperasteekee kleesee
calm	ήσυχος	eeseekhos
camera	η φωτογραφική μηχανή	ee fotoghrafeekee meekhanee
to camp	κατασκηνώνω	kataskeenono
campsite	το κάμπινγκ	to camping
can: I can	μπορώ	boro
you can	μπορείς	borees
he can	μπορεί	boree
we can	μπορούμε	boroome
can (of food)	η κονσέρβα	ee konserva
Canada	ο Καναδάς	o Kanadhas
Canadian	ο Καναδός/ η Καναδή	o Kanadhos/ ee Kanadhee
to cancel	ακυρώνω	akeerono
car	το αυτοκίνητο	to aftokeeneeto
car ferry	το φεριμπότ	to fereebot

English – Greek

English	Greek	Pronunciation
car keys	τα κλειδιά αυτοκινήτου	ta kleedhya aftokeeneetoo
car park	το πάρκινγκ	to parking
card	η κάρτα	ee karta
careful	προσεκτικός	prosekteekos
carriage (railway)	το βαγόνι	to vaghonee
to carry	κουβαλώ	koovalo
to cash (cheque)	εξαργυρώνω	eksaryeerono
cash	τα μετρητά	ta metreeta
cash desk	το ταμείο	to tameeo
cash dispenser	το ATM	to ey tee em
castle	το κάστρο	to kastro
casualty department	τμήμα για επείγοντα περιστατικά	tmeema ya epeeghonda pereestateeka
cat	η γάτα	ee ghata
catalogue	ο κατάλογος	o kataloghos
to catch (bus, train, etc.)	πιάνω	pyano
Catholic	καθολικός	katholikos
cents (euro)	λεπτά	lepta
centimetre	το εκατοστό	to ekastosto
central	κεντρικός	kendreekos
centre	το κέντρο	to kendro
century	ο αιώνας	o eonas
certificate	το πιστοποιη-τικό	to peestopee-ee teeko
chain	η αλυσίδα	ee aleeseedha
chair	η καρέκλα	ee karekla
champagne	η σαμπάνια	ee sambanya
change (money)	η αλλαγή	ee alaghee
to change	τα ρέστα	ta resta
charge (price)	αλλάζω	alazo
charge (electric)	η τιμή	ee teemee
I've run out of charge	η φόρτιση	ee forteesee
cheap	έμεινα από μπαταρία	emeena apo batareea
to check	φτηνός	fteenos
	ελέγχω	elenkho

English	Greek	Pronunciation
to check in	περνώ από τον έλεγχο εισιτηρίων	perno apo ton elenkho eeseeteereeon
cheers!	γεια μας!	ya mas!
cheese	το τυρί	to teeree
chemist's	το φαρμακείο	to farmakeeo
cheque	η επιταγή	ee epeetaghee
cheque card	η κάρτα επιταγών	ee karta epeetaghon
child	το παιδί	to pedhee
children	τα παιδιά	ta pedhya
chips	πατάτες τηγανητές	patates teeghaneetes
chocolate	η σοκολάτα	ee sokolata
Christmas	τα Χριστούγεννα	ta khreestooyena
merry Christmas!	Καλά Χριστούγεννα	kala khreestooyena
church	η εκκλησία	ee ekleseea
cigarette	το τσιγάρο	to tseegharo
cinema	ο κινηματογράφος	o keeneematogh rafos
city	η πόλη	ee polee
clean	καθαρός	katharos
to clean	καθαρίζω	kathareezo
client	ο πελάτης/ η πελάτισσα	o pelatees/ ee pelateesa
climbing	η ορειβασία	ee oreevaseea
clock	το ρολόι	to roloee
to close	κλείνω	kleeno
close adj (near)	κοντινός	kondeenos
close (weather)	αποπνικτικός	apopneekhteekos
closed	κλειστός	kleestos
clothes	τα ρούχα	ta rookha
cloudy	συννεφιασμένος	seenefyasmenos
coach (railway)	το βαγόνι	to vaghonee
coach (bus)	το πούλμαν	to poolman
coach station	ο σταθμός λεωφορείων	o stathmos leoforeeon

English – Greek

English	Greek	pronunciation
coast	η ακτή	ee aktee
coat	το παλτό	to palto
coffee	ο καφές	o kafes
black coffee	σκέτος καφές	sketos kafes
white coffee	καφές με γάλα	kafes me ghala
cold	κρύος	kreeos
I have a cold	είμαι κρυωμένος	eeme kreeomenos
colour	το χρώμα	to khroma
to come	έρχομαι	erkhome
to come back	γυρίζω	yeereezo
to come in	μπαίνω	beno
comfortable	αναπαυτικός	anapafteekos
company (firm)	η εταιρία	ee etereea
compartment (train)	το βαγόνι	to vaghonee
to complain	παραπονούμαι	paraponoome
computer	το κομπιούτερ	to kompyooter
concert	η συναυλία	ee seenavleea
condom	το προφυ-λακτικό	to profeelakteeko
to confirm	επιβεβαιώνω	epeeveveono
congratulations!	συγχαρητήρια	seenkhareetereea
connection (trains; etc)	η σύνδεση	ee seendhesee
consulate	το προξενείο	to prokseneeo
to contact	έρχομαι σε επαφή	erkhome se epafee
contact lenses	οι φακοί επαφής	ee fakee epafees
contraceptives	τα αντισυλ-ληπτικά	ta andeesee-leepteeka
contract	το συμβόλαιο	to seemvoleo
to cook	μαγειρεύω	magheerevo
cooker	η κουζίνα	ee koozeena
cool	δροσερός	dhroseros
to copy (photocopy)	φωτοτυπώ	fototeepo
copy noun	το αντίγραφο	to andeeghrafo

corner	η γωνία	ee ghoneea
cosmetics	τα καλλυντικά	ta kaleendeeka
to cost	κοστίζω	kosteezo
how much does it cost?	πόσο κάνει;	poso kanee;
cough	ο βήχας	o veekhas
country (not town)	η χώρα	ee khora
couple (two people)	το ζευγάρι	to zevgharee
course (meal)	το πιάτο	to pyato
cousin	ο εξάδελφος/ η εξαδέλφη	o eksadhelfos/ ee eksadhelfee
cover charge	το κουβέρ	to koover
to crash	συγκρούομαι	seengkrooome
crash	η σύγκρουση	ee seengkroosee
crash helmet	το κράνος	to kranos
credit (on mobile phone)	οι μονάδες	ee monadhes

credit card	η πιστωτική κάρτα	ee peestoteekee karta
to cross	διασχίζω	dheeaskheezo
crowded	γεμάτος	yematos
cruise	η κρουαζιέρα	ee krooazyera
cup	το φλυτζάνι	to fleedzanee
current (electric)	το ρεύμα	to revma
customer	ο πελάτης	o pelatees
to cut	κόβω	kovo
to cycle	ποδηλατώ	podheelato
cystitis	η κυστίτιδα	ee keesteeteedha

D

daily	ημερήσιος	eemereeseeos
dairy products	τα γαλακτοκομικά προϊόντα	ta ghalaktoko-meeka proeeonda
damage	η ζημιά	ee zeemya
damp	υγρός	eeghros
dance	ο χορός	o khoros

English	Greek	Pronunciation
to dance	χορεύω	khorevo
danger	ο κίνδυνος	o keendheenos
dangerous	επικίνδυνος	epeekeendheenos
dark (colour)	σκούρο	skooro
date	η ημερομηνία	ee eemeromee-neea
date of birth	η ημερομηνία γεννήσεως	ee eemeromee-neea yeneeseos
daughter	η κόρη	ee koree
day	η μέρα	ee mera
dead	νεκρός	nekros
dear (expensive)	αγαπητός	aghapeetos
debit card	η κάρτα αναλήψεις	ee karta analeepsees
decaffeinated	χωρίς καφεΐνη	khorees kafe-eenee
deck chair	η ξαπλώστρα	ee ksaplostra
deep	βαθύς	vathees
delay	η καθυστέρηση	ee katheesteresee

English	Greek	Pronunciation
delayed	καθυστερη-μένος	katheesteree-menos
delicious	νόστιμος	nosteemos
dentist	ο/η οδοντία-τρος	o/ee odhondee-atros
deodorant	το αποσμητικό	to aposmeeteeko
department store	το πολυκατά-στημα	to poleekata-steema
departure	η αναχώρηση	ee anakhoreesee
diabetic	διαβητικός	dheeaveeteekos
to dial	παίρνω αριθμό	perno areethmo
dialling code	ο τηλεφωνικός κώδικας	o teelefoneekos kodheekas
diet	η δίαιτα	ee dhee-eta
I'm on a diet	κάνω δίαιτα	kano dhee-eta
different	διαφορετικός	dheeaforeteekos
difficult	δύσκολος	dheeskolos
digital camera	η ψηφιακή φωτογραφική μηχανή	ee psefeeakee fotoghrafeekee meekhanee

English	Greek	pronunciation
dining room	η τραπεζαρία	ee trapezaree
dinner	το δείπνο	to dheepno
direct	άμεσος	amesos
directory (telephone)	ο τηλεφωνικός κατάλογος	o teelefoneekos kataloghos
dirty	βρώμικος	vromeekos
disabled	ανάπηρος	anapeeros
discount	η έκπτωση	ee ekptosee
divorced	χωρισμένος/ χωρισμένη	khoreesmenos/ khoreesmene
dizzy	ζαλισμένος	zaleesmenos
to do: I do	κάνω	kano
you do	κάνεις	kanes
doctor	ο/ε γιατρός	o/e yatros
documents	τα έγγραφα	ta engrafa
dog	το σκυλί	to skeelee
dollar	το δολάριο	to dholareeo
door	η πόρτα	ee porta
double	διπλός	dheeplos
double bed	το διπλό κρεββάτι	to dheeplo krevvate
double room	το δίκλινο δωμάτιο	to dheekleeno dhomateeo
down: to go down	κατεβαίνω	kateveno
downstairs	κάτω	kato
dress	το φόρεμα	to forema
to dress	ντύνομαι	deenome
drink noun	το ποτό	to poto
to have a drink	παίρνω ένα ποτό	perno ena poto
to drink	πίνω	peeno
drinking water	το πόσιμο νερό	to poseemo nero
to drive	οδηγώ	odheegho
driver	ο οδηγός	o odheeghos
driving licence	η άδεια οδήγησης	ee adheea odheegheesees
to drown	πνίγομαι	pneeghome

English – Greek

English – Greek

English	Greek	Pronunciation
drug (illegal)	το ναρκωτικό	to narkoteeko
(medicine)	το φάρμακο	to farmako
drunk	μεθυσμένος	metheesmenos
dry adj	στεγνός	steghnos
to dry	στεγνώνω	steghnono
dry-cleaners	το καθαρι-	to kathareestee-
	στήριο	reeo
during	κατά τη	kata tee
	διάρκεια	dheearkeea
E		
each	κάθε	kathe
ear	το αυτί	to aftee
earache: I have	με πονάει το	me ponaee to
earache	αυτί μου	aftee moo
earlier	νωρίτερα	noreetera
early	νωρίς	norees
east	η ανατολή	ee anatolee
Easter	το Πάσχα	to paskha
easy	εύκολος	efkolos

English	Greek	Pronunciation
to eat	τρώω	troo
electronic	ηλεκτρονικός/-	eelektroneekos/-
	ή/ό	ee/o
e-mail	το e-mail	to e-mail
e-mail address	η e-mail	ee e-mail
	διεύθυνση	dheeeftheensee
embassy	η πρεσβεία	ee presveea
emergency: it's	είναι επείγον	eene epeeghon
an emergency	περιστατικό	pereestateeko
empty	άδειος	adheeos
end	το τέλος	to telos
engaged	αρραβωνια-	aravonyas
(to marry)	σμένος/η	menos/ee
engine	η μηχανή	ee meekhanee
England	η Αγγλία	ee angleea
English (thing)	αγγλικός	angleekos
Englishman/	ο Άγγλος/	o anglos/
woman	η Αγγλίδα	ee angleedha
to enjoy oneself	διασκεδάζω	dhyaskedhazo
enough	αρκετά	arketa

English	Greek	Pronunciation
enough bread	αρκετό ψωμί	arketo psomee
enquiry desk/office	το γραφείο πληροφοριών	to ghrafeeo pleeroforeon
to enter	μπαίνω	beno
entrance	η είσοδος	ee eesodhos
entrance fee	η τιμή εισόδου	ee teemee eesodhou
essential	απαραίτητος	apareeteetos
euro	ευρώ	evro
Europe	η Ευρώπη	ee evropee
evening	το βράδυ	to vradhee
this evening	απόψε	apopse
in the evening	το βράδυ	to vradhee
every	κάθε	kathe
everyone	όλοι	olee
everything	όλα	ola
excellent	εξαιρετικός	eksereteekos
except	εκτός από	ektos apo
exchange rate	η τιμή του συναλλάγματος	ee teemee too seenalaghmatos
excuse me	με συγχωρείτε	me seeghkhoreete
exit	η έξοδος	ee eksodhos
expensive	ακριβός	akreevos
extra: it costs	κοστίζει	kosteezee
extra	επιπλέον	epeepleon
extra money	περισσότερα χρήματα	pereesotera khreemata
eyes	τα μάτια	ta matya
F		
face	το πρόσωπο	to prosopo
facilities	οι ευκολίες	ee efkoleeyes
to faint	λιποθυμώ	leepotheemo
to fall	πέφτω	pefto
he/she has fallen	έπεσε	epese
family	η οικογένεια	ee eekoyeneea
fan (electric)	ο ανεμιστήρας	o anemeesteeras
far	μακριά	makreea
fare (bus, train)	το εισιτήριο	to eeseeteereeo

English – Greek

fast	γρήγορα	ghreeghora	film (for camera)	το φιλμ	to feelm
father	ο πατέρας	o pateras	(in cinema)	η ταινία	ee teneea
fault (mistake)	το λάθος	to lathos	to finish	τελειώνω	teleeono
it is not my fault	δε φταίω εγώ	dhe fteo egho	fire (heater)	η θερμάστρα	ee thermastra
fax	το φαξ	to fax	Fire!	φωτιά!	fotya!
to feel	αισθάνομαι	esthanome	fire brigade	η πυροσβεσ-	ee peerosvesteeke
I feel sick	θέλω να κάνω	thelo na kano		τική	
	εμετό	emeto	fire extinguisher	ο πυροσβεσ-	o peerosvesteeras
female	θηλυκός	theeleekos		τήρας	
ferry	το φέριμπότ	to fereebot	first	πρώτος	protos
to fetch	φέρνω	ferno	first aid	οι πρώτες	ee protes
fever	ο πυρετός	o peeretos		βοήθειες	voeetheeyes
fiance(e)	ο αρραβωνια-	o aravon-	first class (seat, etc)	η πρώτη θέση	ee protee thesee
	στικός/	steekos/	first name	το όνομα	to onoma
	η αρραβωνια-	ee aravon-	fish	το ψάρι	to psaree
	στικιά	yasteekya	to fit (healthy)	υγιής	eeyees
to fill	γεμίζω	yemeezo	to fix (arrange)	φτιάχνω	ftyakhno
fill it up! (car)	γεμίστε το	yemeeste to	fizzy (drink)	κανονίζω	kanoneezo
fillet	το φιλέτο	to feeleto		αεριούχο	aeryoukho

English	Greek	
flat (apartment)	το διαμέρισμα	to dheeame-reesma
flight	η πτήση	ee pteesee
floor (storey)	το πάτωμα	to patoma
flower	ο όροφος	o orofos
	το λουλούδι	to looloodhee
flu	η γρίππη	ee ghreepee
to fly	πετώ	peto
food	το φαγητό	to fa-yeeto
food poisoning	η τροφική δηλητηρίαση	ee trofeekee dhee-leeteereeasee
foot	το πόδι	to podhee
football	το ποδόσφαιρο	to podhosfero
for	για	ya
foreign	ξένος	ksenos
to forget	ξεχνώ	ksekhno
fork (in road)	το πηρούνι	to peeroonee
	το κατάγμα	to kataghma
fracture (of bone)	το διακλάδωση	ee dheeakladhosee
France	η Γαλλία	ee ghaleea

English	Greek	
free	ελεύθερος	eleftheros
(costing nothing)	δωρεάν	dhorean
French (thing)	γαλλικός	ghaleekos
frequent	συχνός	seekhnos
fresh	φρέσκος	freskos
fried	τηγανητός	teeghaneetos
friend	ο φίλος/η φίλη	o feelos/ee feelee
from	από	apo
front (part)	το μπροστινό	to brosteeno
	(μέρος)	(meros)
in front	μπροστά	brosta
fruit	τα φρούτα	ta froota
fruit juice	ο χυμός φρούτων	o kheemos frooton
full	γεμάτος	yematos
full board	(η) πλήρης διατροφή	(ee) pleerees dheeatrofee
funny	αστείος	asteeos

G

gallery (art)	η πινακοθήκη	ee peenakothee-kee
game (to eat)	το παιγνίδι	to peghneedhee
garage (for parking car)	το κυνήγι	to keeneeghee
garden	ο κήπος	o keepos
gate (at airport)	η έξοδος	ee eksodhos
gents (toilet)	ανδρών	andhron
genuine	γνήσιος	ghneeseeos
to get (fetch)	παίρνω	perno
to get in (car, etc.)	φέρνω	ferno
to get off (from bus)	μπαίνω	beno
	κατεβαίνω από	kateveno apo
to get on (bus)	ανεβαίνω στο	aneveno sto
	λεωφορείο	leoforeeo
gift	το δώρο	to dhoro
girl	το κορίτσι	to koreetsee

girlfriend	η φίλη/	ee feelee/
	η φιλενάδα	ee feelenadha
to give	δίνω	dheeno
glass (to drink from)	το ποτήρι	to poteree
a glass of water	ένα ποτήρι νερό	ena poteree nero
glasses (spectacles)	τα γυαλιά	ta yalya
to go	πηγαίνω	peegheno
I go/I am going	πηγαίνω	peegheno
you go/you are going	πηγαίνεις	peeghenees
we go/we are going	πηγαίνουμε	peeghenoome
to go back	γυρίζω πίσω	yeereezo peeso
to go in	μπαίνω	beno
to go out	βγαίνω	vyeno
gold	ο χρυσός	o khreesos
(made of gold)	χρυσός	khreesos

good	καλός	kalos	group	η ομάδα	ee omadha
good afternoon	χαίρετε	kherete	guest	ο φιλοξενού-	o feeloksenoo
goodbye	αντίο	adeeo		μενος	menos
good day	καλημέρα	kaleemera	o/η ξεναγός	o/ee ksenaghos
good evening	καλησπέρα	kaleespera	guide	ο οδηγός	o odheeghos
good morning	καλημέρα	kaleemera	guidebook		
good night	καληνύχτα	kaleeneekhta			
grandfather	ο παππούς	o papoos	**H**		
grandmother	η γιαγιά	ee yaya	hair	τα μαλλιά	ta malya
grapes	τα σταφύλια	ta stafeelya	hairdresser	ο κομμωτής/	o komotees/
great	μεγάλος	meghalos		η κομμώτρια	ee komotreea
Greece	η Ελλάδα	ee eladha	half	το μισό	to meeso
Greek (person)	ο Έλληνας/	o eleenas/	half an hour	μισή ώρα	meesee ora
	η Ελληνίδα	ee eleeneedha	half board	(η) ημιδιατροφή	(ee) eemeedhee-
Greek adj	ελληνικός	eleeneekos			atrofee
green	πράσινος	praseenos	half price	μισή τιμή	meesee teemee
grey	γκρίζος	greezos	hand	το χέρι	to kheree
grocer's	το μπακάλικο	to bakaleeko	handbag	η τσάντα	ee tsanda
	το παντοπω-	to pandopoleeo	handicapped	ανάπηρος	anapeeros
	λείο				

handkerchief (tissue)	το μαντήλι	to mandeelee	hello	γεια σας	ya sas
	το χαρτομά-ντηλο	to khartoman-deelo	to help	βοηθώ	voeetho
hand luggage	η χειραποσκευή	ee kheeraposkevee	help!	βοήθεια	voeetheea
hand-made	χειροποίητος	kheeropee-eetos	here	εδώ	edho
to happen	συμβαίνω	seemveno	to hire	νοικιάζω	neekyazo
what happened?	τι συνέβη;	tee seenevee?	to hold	κρατώ	krato
happy	χαρούμενος	kharoomenos	hold-up	ο καθυστέρηση	ee katheestereesee
hard (difficult)	δύσκολος	dheeskolos	holidays	οι διακοπές	ee dheeakopes
hat	το καπέλο	to kapelo	home	το σπίτι	sto speetee
he	αυτός	aftos	at home	στο σπίτι	sto speetee
head	το κεφάλι	to kefalee	to hope	ελπίζω	elpeezo
headache: I have a headache	έχω πονοκέ-φαλο	ekho ponokefalo	hospital	το νοσοκομείο	to nosokomeeo
health	η υγεία	ee eegheea	hot	ζεστός	zestos
to hear	ακούω	akoo-o	I'm hot	ζεσταίνομαι	zestenome
heart	η καρδιά	ee kardhya	it's hot	έχει ζέστη	ekhee zestee
heating	η θέρμανση	ee thermansee	hot water	το ζεστό νερό	to zesto nero
heavy	βαρύς	varees	hotel	το ξενοδοχείο	to ksenodhokheeo
			hour	η ώρα	ee ora
			house	το σπίτι	to speetee
			house wine	το κρασί χύμα	to krasee kheema

English	Greek	Pronunciation
how	πώς	pos
how long?	πόση ώρα;	posee ora?
how much?	πόσο;	poso?
how many?	πόσα;	posa?
how are you?	πώς είστε;	pos eeste?
I'm hungry	πεινώ	peeno
to hurry: I'm in a hurry	βιάζομαι	vyazome
to hurt: that hurts	με πονάει	me ponaee
husband	ο σύζυγος	o seezeeghos
I	εγώ	egho
ice	ο πάγος	o paghos
ice cream/ ice lolly	το παγωτό	to paghoto
if	αν	an
ill	άρρωστος	arostos
immediately	αμέσως	amesos
impossible	αδύνατο	adheenato
in (inside)	μέσα	mesa
(into)	σε	se
(with countries, towns)	στο/ στη/ στο	sto/ stee/ sto
infectious	μεταδοτικός	metadhoteekos
information	οι πληροφορίες	ee pleeroforeeyes
injured	τραυματισμένος	travmateesmenos
insect	το έντομο	to endomo
inside (interior)	το εσωτερικό	to esotereeko
inside the car	μέσα στο αυτοκίνητο	mesa sto aftokeeneeto
it's inside	είναι μέσα	eene mesa
insurance	η ασφάλεια	ee asfalea
insured	ασφαλισμένος	asfaleesmenos
interesting	ενδιαφέρων	endheeaferon
international	διεθνής	dhee-ethnees

English – Greek

to invite	προσκαλώ	proskalo	
Ireland	η Ιρλανδία	ee eerlandheea	
Irish (person)	ο Ιρλανδός/	o eerlandhos/	
	η Ιρλανδή	ee eerlandhee	
iron (for clothes)	το σίδερο	to seedhero	
island	το νησί	to neesee	
it	το	to	
Italy	η Ιταλία	ee eetaleea	
itch	η φαγούρα	ee faghoora	

J

jacket	το μπουφάν	to boofan	
jam	η μαρμελάδα	ee marmeladha	
jar	το βάζο	to vazo	
jeans	το τζιν	to jean	
jeweller's	το κοσμηματο-	to kosmeemato-	
	πωλείο	poleeo	
jewellery	τα κοσμήματα	ta kosmeemata	
job	η δουλειά	ee dhoolya	
joke	το αστείο	to asteeo	

journey	το ταξίδι	to takseedhee
juice	ο χυμός	o kheemos
just: *just two*	μόνο δύο	mono dheeo
I've just arrived	μόλις έρτασα	molees eftasa

K

to keep	κρατώ	krato
key	το κλειδί	to kleedhee
kilo	το κιλό	to keelo
kilometre	το χιλιόμετρο	to kheelyometro
kind (sort)	το είδος	to eedhos
kind (adj)	ευγενικός	ef-gheneekos
kiosk	το περίπτερο	to pereeptero
kitchen	η κουζίνα	ee koozeena
knife	το μαχαίρι	to makheree
to knock down (by car)	χτυπώ με αυτοκίνητο	khteepo me aftokeeneeto

L

ladies (toilet)	γυναικών	yeenekon

English	Greek	
lady	η κυρία	ee keereea
lager	η μπίρα	ee beera
lamb	το αρνάκι	to arnakee
lamp	η λάμπα	ee lamba
to land (plane)	προσγειώνω	prosgheeono
language	η γλώσσα	ee ghlosa
large	μεγάλος	meghalos
last	τελευταίος	telefteos
late (in the day)	αργά	argha
I am late (for an appointment)	έχω αργήσει	ekho argheesee
later	αργότερα	arghotera
lavatory	η τουαλέτα	ee tooaleta
lazy	τεμπέλης	tembelees
to learn	μαθαίνω	matheno
leather	το δέρμα	to dherma
to leave (go away)	φεύγω	fevgho
left: (on/to the) left	αριστερά	areestera

English	Greek	
left-luggage (office)	η φύλαξη αποσκευών	ee feelaksee aposkevon
leg	το πόδι	to podhee
lemon	το λεμόνι	to lemonee
lemonade	η λεμονάδα	ee lemonadha
lens	ο φακός	o fakos
less: less milk	λιγότερο γάλα	leeghotero ghala
lesson	το μάθημα	to matheema
to let (allow) (hire out)	επιτρέπω	epeetrepo
letter	νοικιάζω	neekyazo
licence	το γράμμα	to ghrama
to lie down	η άδεια	ee adheea
lift	ξαπλώνω	ksaplono
light	το ασανσέρ	to asanser
line	το φως	to fos
to like: I like	μου αρέσει	moo aresee
listen	η γραμμή	ee ghramee
to listen	ακούω	akoo-o
litre	το λίτρο	to leetro

English	Greek	Pronunciation
little	μικρός	meekros
a little	λίγο	leegho
to live	μένω	meno
he lives in London	μένει στο Λονδίνο	menee sto londeeno
lock	η κλειδαριά	ee kleedharya
to lock	κλειδώνω	kleedhono
I'm locked out	κλειδώθηκα έξω	kleedhotheeka ekso
London	το Λονδίνο	to londheeno
long	μακρύς	makrees
to look at	κοιτάζω	keetazo
to look after	φροντίζω	frondeezo
to lose	χάνω	khano
lost	χαμένος	khamenos
I've lost my wallet	έχασα το πορτοφόλι μου	ekhasa to portofolee moo
I am lost	χάθηκα	khatheeka
lost-property office	το γραφείο απωλεσθέντων αντικειμένων	to ghrafeeo apolesthendon andeekeemenon
lot: a lot (of)	πολύς	polees
loud	δυνατός	dheenatos
to love	αγαπώ	aghapo
low	χαμηλός	khameelos
luggage	οι αποσκευές	ee aposkeves
lunch	το μεσημεριανό	to meseemeryano

M

machine	η μηχανή	ee meekhanee
mad	τρελός	trelos
magazine	το περιοδικό	to pereeodheeko
main course (of meal)	το κύριο πιάτο	to keereeo pyato
to make	κάνω	kano
make-up	το μακιγιάζ	to makeeyaz
male	αρσενικός	arseneekos

man	ο άντρας	o andras
manager	ο διαχειριστής	o dheeakheereestees
many	πολλοί	polee
many people	πολλοί άνθρωποι	polee anthropee
map	ο χάρτης	o khartees
market	η αγορά	ee aghora
married	παντρεμένος	pandremenos
material	το υλικό	to eeleeko
matter: *it doesn't matter*	δεν πειράζει	dhen peerazee
what's the matter with you?	τι έχεις;	tee ekhees?
meal	το γεύμα	to yevma
meat	το κρέας	to kreas
medicine (drug)	το φάρμακο	to farmako
Mediterranean	η Μεσόγειος	ee mesoyeeos
to meet	συναντώ	seenando

English – Greek

meeting	η συνάντηση	ee seenandeese
melon (watermelon)	το πεπόνι	to peponee
	το καρπούζι	to karpoozee
men	οι άντρες	ee andres
menu	ο κατάλογος/	o kataloghos/
	το μενού	to menoo
message	το μήνυμα	to meeneema
metre	το μέτρο	to metro
midday	το μεσημέρι	to meseemeree
midnight	τα μεσάνυχτα	ta mesaneekhta
milk	το γάλα	to ghala
millimetre	το χιλιοστό-μετρο	to kheelyosto-metro
to mind: *do you mind if…?*	σας ενοχλεί αν…;	sas enokhlee an…?
minute	το λεπτό	to lepto
to miss (train, etc.)	χάνω	khano
Miss	η Δεσποινίς	ee dhespeenees
missing	χαμένος	khamenos
he's missing	λείπει	leepee

mistake	το λάθος	to lathos	Mrs	Κυρία	keereea
mobile (phone)	το κινητό	to keeneeto	much	πολύς	polees
	(τηλέφωνο)	(teelefono)	too much	πάρα πολύ	para polee
mobile number	ο αριθμός	o areethmos	very much	πάρα πολύ	para polee
	κινητού	keeneetoo	museum	το μουσείο	to mooseeo
money	τα χρήματα/	ta khreemata/	music	η μουσική	ee mooseekee
	τα λεφτά	ta lefta	must: I must go	πρέπει να πάω	prepee na pao
month	ο μήνας	o meenas	you must go	πρέπει να πας	prepee na pas
more	περισσότερο	pereesotero	he/she must go	πρέπει να πάει	prepee na paee
more bread	κι άλλο ψωμί	kee alo psomee	we must go	πρέπει να πάμε	prepee na pame
morning	το πρωί	to proee			
most	το περισσότερο	to pereesotero	**N**		
mother	η μητέρα	ee meetera	name	το όνομα	to onoma
motor	η μηχανή	ee meekhanee	narrow	στενός	stenos
motorbike	η μοτοσικλέτα	ee motoseekleta	near	κοντά	konda
motorway	ο αυτοκινητό-	o aftokeeneeto-	nationality	η υπηκοότητα	ee eepeeko-oteeta
	δρομος	dhromos	necessary	απαραίτητος	apareeteetos
mouth	το στόμα	to stoma	to need: I need...	χρειάζομαι...	khreeazome...
to move	κινούμαι	keenoome	never	ποτέ	pote
Mr	Κύριος	keereeos	new	καινούριος	kenooryos

English – Greek

English	Greek	Pronunciation
news (TV, radio)	οι ειδήσεις	ee eedheesees
newspaper	η εφημερίδα	ee efeemereedha
New Year; happy New Year!	καλή χρονιά!	kalee khronya!
New Zealand	η Νέα Ζηλανδία	ee nea zeeland-heea
next	επόμενος	epomenos
nice (thing)	ωραίος	oreos
(person)	καλός	kalos
night	η νύχτα	ee neekhta
no	όχι	okhee
nobody	κανένας	kanenas
noise	ο θόρυβος	o thoreevos
non-alcoholic	μη οινοπνευ-ματώδης	mee eenopnev-matodhees
none	κανένα	kanena
non-smoking	μη καπνίζοντες	mee kapnee-zondes
north	ο βορράς	o voras
nose	η μύτη	ee meetee
not	μη/ δεν	mee/ dhen
I am not	δεν είμαι	dhen eeme
don't stop	μη σταματάτε	mee stamatas
nothing	τίποτα	teepota
now	τώρα	tora
number	ο αριθμός	o areethmos
O		
off (light, machine, etc)	σβηστός	sveestos
it's off (rotten)	είναι χαλασ-μένο	eene khalasmeno
office	το γραφείο	to ghrafeeo
often	συχνά	seekhna
OK	εντάξει	endaksee
old (person)	ηλικιωμένος	eeleekyomenos
(thing)	παλιός	palyos

English	Greek	Pronunciation
how old are you?	πόσων χρονών είστε;	poson khronon eeste?
on (on top of)	πάνω	pano
on (light, TV)	ανοιχτός	aneekhtos
on the table	(πάνω) στο τραπέζι	(pano) sto trapezee
once	μία φορά	meea fora
only	μόνο	mono
to open	ανοίγω	aneegho
open adj	ανοιχτός	aneektos
opposite	απέναντι	apenandee
or	ή	ee
to order	παραγγέλλω	parang-elo
Orthodox (religion)	ορθόδοξος	orthodhoksos
other	άλλος	alos
out (light, etc.)	σβηστός	sveesmenos
he's out	λείπει	leepee
outside	έξω	ekso
over	πάνω από	pano apo
over there	εκεί πέρα	ekee pera

English	Greek	Pronunciation
to owe: you owe me	μου χρωστάς	moo khrostas
P		
package tour	η οργανωμένη εκδρομή	ee orghanomene ekdhromee
paid	πληρωμένος	pleeromenos
pain	ο πόνος	o ponos
painful	οδυνηρός	odheeneros
it's painful	πονάει	ponaee
painting	ο πίνακας	o peenakas
pair	το ζευγάρι	to zevgharee
pan	η κατσαρόλα	ee katsarola
paper	το χαρτί	to khartee
parcel	το δέμα	to dhema
pardon	παρακαλώ	parakalo
I beg your pardon	με συγχωρείτε	me seenkhoreete
parents	οι γονείς	o ghonees
park noun	το πάρκο	to parko

English	Greek	pronunciation
to park (in car)	παρκάρω	parkaro
part	το μέρος	to meros
passenger	ο επιβάτης	o epeevatees
passport control	ο έλεγχος διαβατηρίων	o elenghos dheeavateereeon
pasta	τα ζυμαρικά	ta zeemareeka
to pay	πληρώνω	pleerono
payment	η πληρωμή	ee pleeromee
pen	το στυλό	to steelo
pensioner	ο/η συνταξιούχος	o/ee seendaks-yookhos
pepper (spice) (vegetable)	το πιπέρι η πιπεριά	to peeperee ee peeperya
per; per hour	την ώρα	teen ora
perfect	τέλειος	teleeos
performance	η παράσταση	ee parastasee
perhaps	ίσως	eesos
person	το άτομο	to atomo
petrol	η βενζίνη	ee venzeenee

English	Greek	pronunciation
petrol station	το βενζινάδικο/ το πρατήριο βενζίνης	to venzeenadheeko/ to prateereeo venzeenees
pharmacist	ο φαρμακοποιός	o farmakopeeos
phonecard	η τηλεκάρτα	ee teelekarta
photocopy	η φωτοτυπία	ee fototeepeea
photograph	η φωτογραφία	ee fotoghrafeea
pie	η πίτα	ee peeta
pillow	το μαξιλάρι	to makseelaree
platform	η αποβάθρα	ee apovathra
to play	παίζω	pezo
please	παρακαλώ	parakalo
pleased	ευχαριστημένος	efkhareestee-menos
police	η αστυνομία	ee asteenomeea
policeman	ο αστυνόμος	o asteenomos
police station	το αστυνομικό τμήμα	to asteenomeeko tmeema

English – Greek

English	Greek	Pronunciation
pool (for swimming)	η πισίνα	ee peeseena
pork	το χοιρινό	to kheereeno
port (harbour)	το λιμάνι	to leemanee
to post (letter)	ταχυδρομώ	takheedhromo
postcard	η καρτποστάλ	ee kartpostal
postcode	ο κωδικός	o kodheekos
post office	το ταχυδρομείο	to takheedhromeeo
pound (money)	η λίρα	ee leera
to prefer	προτιμώ	proteemo
pregnant	έγγυος	engeeos
to prepare	ετοιμάζω	eteemazo
prescription	η συνταγή	ee sendaghee
present (gift)	το δώρο	to dhoro
pretty	ωραίος	oreos
price	η τιμή	ee teemee
price list	ο τιμοκατάλογος	o teemokataloghos
private	ιδιωτικός	eedheeoteekos

English	Greek	Pronunciation
problem	το πρόβλημα	to provleema
prohibited	απαγορευμένος	apaghorevmenos
to pronounce	προφέρω	profero
how do you pronounce this?	πώς το προφέρετε;	pos to proferete?
public	δημόσιος	dheemoseeos
public holiday	η γιορτή	ee yortee
purse	το πορτοφόλι	to portofolee
to push	σπρώχνω	sprokhno
to put	βάζω	vazo
to put down	βάζω κάτω	vazo kato
Q		
quality	η ποιότητα	ee peeoteeta
question	η ερώτηση	ee eroteesee
queue	η ουρά	ee oora
quick	γρήγορος	ghreeghoros
quickly	γρήγορα	ghreeghora

quiet	ήσυχος	eeseekhos

R

radio	το ραδιόφωνο	to radhyofono
railway station	ο σιδηρόδρο-μικός σταθμός	o seedheerodhro-meekos stathmos
rain	η βροχή	ee vrokhee
raining; it's raining	βρέχει	vrekhee
rare	σπάνιος	spanyos
(steak)	μισοψημένος	meesopseemenos
rate	ο ρυθμός	o reethmos
rate of exchange	η ισοτιμία	ee eesoteemeea
raw	ωμός	omos
razor	το ξυράφι	to kseerafee
to read	διαβάζω	dheeavazo
ready	έτοιμος	eteemos
real	πραγματικός	praghmateekos
receipt	η απόδειξη	ee apodheeksee
reception (desk)	η ρεσεψιόν	ee resepsyon

to recommend	συνιστώ	seeneesto
red	κόκκινος	kokeenos
reduction	η έκπτωση	ee ekptosee
refund	η επιστροφή χρημάτων	ee epeestrofee khreematon
registered (letter)	συστημένο	seestemeeno
relations (family)	οι συγγενείς	ee seenghenees
to relax	ξεκουράζομαι	ksekoorazome
to remember	θυμάμαι	theemame
to rent	νοικιάζω	neekyazo
to repair	επιδιορθώνω	epedheeorthono
to repeat	επαναλαμβάνω	epanalamvano
reservation	η κράτηση	ee krateesee
to reserve	κρατώ	krato
reserved	κρατημένος	krateemenos
rest	ξεκούραση	ksekoorasee
the rest (the others)	οι υπόλοιποι	ee eepoleepee
to rest	ξεκουράζομαι	ksekoorazome
restaurant	το εστιατόριο	to esteeatoreeo

English – Greek

English	Greek	Pronunciation
retired	συνταξιούχος	seendaksyookhos
to return (go back, give back)	επιστρέφω	epeestrefo
return ticket	το εισιτήριο με το επιστροφή	to eeseeteereeo me epeestrofee
rice	το ρύζι	to reezee
rich (person, food)	πλούσιος	plooseeos
right (correct, accurate)	σωστός	sostos
(on/to the) right	δεξιά	dheksya
road	ο δρόμος	o dhromos
road map	ο οδικός χάρτης	o odheekos khartees
roast	το ψητό	to pseeto
room (in house, etc.)	το δωμάτιο	to dhomateeo
(space)	ο χώρος	o khoros
rosé	ροζέ	roze
round (shape)	στρογγυλός	strongeelos

English	Greek	Pronunciation
round Greece	γύρω στην Ελλάδα	yeero steen eladha
to run	τρέχω	trekho

S

sad	λυπημένος	leepeemenos
safe adj (harmless)	αβλαβής	avlaves
(not dangerous)	ακίνδυνος	akeendheenos
(secure, sure)	ασφαλής	asfalees
salad	το σαλάτα	ee salata
salt	το αλάτι	to alatee
same	ίδιος	eedhyos
sand	η άμμος	ee amos
sauce	η σάλτσα	ee saltsa
to say	λέω	leo
Scotland	η Σκωτία	ee skotea
Scottish (person)	ο Σκωτσέζος/ η Σκωτσέζα	o skotsezos/ ee skotseza
sculpture	το γλυπτό	to ghleepto
sea	η θάλασσα	ee thalasa

English	Greek	Pronunciation	English	Greek	Pronunciation
seafood	τα θαλασσινά	ta thalaseena	shirt	το πουκάμισο	to pookameeso
seaside (beach, seafront)	η παραλία	ee paralea	shoe	το παπούτσι	to papootsee
seat (in theatre)	η θέση	ee thesee	to shop	ψωνίζω	psoneezo
second	δεύτερος	dhefteros	shop	το μαγαζί	to maghazee
to see	βλέπω	vlepo	short	κοντός	kondos
to sell	πουλώ	poolo	show (in theatre, etc.)	η παράσταση	ee parastasee
to send	στέλνω	stelno	to show	δείχνω	dheekhno
to serve	σερβίρω	serveero	shower (in bath)	το ντους	to doos
service (in restaurant, etc.)	η εξυπηρέτηση	ee exseepeereeteesee	shower (rain)	η μπόρα	ee bora
shallow	ρηχός	reekhos	shut (closed)	κλειστός	kleestos
shampoo	το σαμπουάν	to sambooan	to shut	κλείνω	kleeno
to share	μοιράζω	meerazo	sick (ill)	άρρωστος	arostos
shaver	η ξυριστική μηχανή	ee kseereesteekee meekhanee	to be sick (vomit)	κάνω εμετό	kano emeto
she	αυτή	aftee	sign (roadsign, notice, etc.)	η πινακίδα	ee peenakeedha
sheet	το σεντόνι	to sendone	signature	η υπογραφή	ee eepoghrafee
ship	το πλοίο	to pleeo	silver	ασημένιος	aseemenyos
			to sing	τραγουδώ	traghoodho
			single (not married)	ελεύθερος	eleftheros

single bed	το μονό κρεβάτι	to mono krevatee	soap	το σαπούνι	to sapoonee
single room	το μονόκλινο δωμάτιο	to monokleeno dhomateeo	soft drink	το αναψυκτικό	to anapseekteeko
sister	η αδελφή	ee adhelfee	some	μερικοί	mereekee
to sit (down)	κάθομαι	kathome	someone	κάποιος	kapyos
size (of clothes, shoes)	το νούμερο	to noomero	something	κάτι	katee
			sometimes	κάποτε	kapote
skin	το δέρμα	to dherma	son	ο γιος	o yos
skirt	η φούστα	ee foosta	song	το τραγούδι	to traghoodhee
sky	ο ουρανός	o ooranos	as soon as possible	σύντομα	seendoma
to sleep	κοιμούμαι	keemoome	sooner	το συντομότερο	to seendomotero
slice	η φέτα	ee feta	sorry: I'm sorry (apology)	νωρίτερα	noreetera
slow	αργά	argha		συγγνώμη	seeghnomee
small	μικρός	meekros	soup	η σούπα	ee soopa
smell	η μυρωδιά	ee meerodhya	south	ο νότος	o notos
smile	το χαμόγελο	to khamoyelo	to speak	μιλώ	meelo
to smile	χαμογελώ	khamoyelo	special	ειδικός	eedheekos
smoke	ο καπνός	o kapnos	special needs	ειδικές ανάγκες	eedheekes anangkes
to smoke	καπνίζω	kapneezo			
snow	το χιόνι	to khyonee			

English	Greek	
speed	η ταχύτητα	ee takheeteeta
speed limit	το όριο ταχύτητας	to oreeo takheeteetas
spirits	τα οινοπνευμ- ατώδη ποτά	ta eenopnev- matodhee pota
spoon	το κουτάλι	to kootalee
sport	το σπορ	to spor
spring (season)	η άνοιξη	ee aneeksee
square (in town)	η πλατεία	ee plateea
stamp	το γραμματό- σημο	to ghramato- seemo
to start	αρχίζω	arkheezo
starter (in meal)	το ορεκτικό	to orekteeko
station	ο σταθμός	o stathmos
to stay	μένω	meno
steak	η μπριτζόλα	ee breezola
sterling	η αγγλική λίρα	ee angleekee leera

English	Greek	
still (yet)	ακόμα	akoma
(immobile)	ακίνητος	akeeneetos
(water)	μη αεριούχο	mee aereeookho
to stop	σταματώ	stamato
straight:	ευθεία	eftheea
straight on		
strawberry	η φράουλα	ee fraoola
street	ο δρόμος	o dhromos
street plan	ο οδικός χάρτης	o odheekos khartees
strong	δυνατός	dheenatos
student	ο φοιτητής/ η φοιτήτρια	o feeteetees/ ee feeteetreea
sugar	η ζάχαρη	ee zakharee
suitcase	η βαλίτσα	ee valeetsa
summer	το καλοκαίρι	to kalokeree
sun	ο ήλιος	o eeleeos
to sunbathe	κάνω ηλιοθε- ραπεία	kano eeleeothera- peea

English – Greek

English – Greek

English	Greek	Pronunciation
sunburn (painful)	το κάψιμο από τον ήλιο	to kapseemo apo ton eeleeo
suncream	η αντιηλιακή κρέμα	ee andee-eeleeakee krema
sunglasses	τα γυαλιά του ήλιου	ta yalya too eeleeoo
sunny (weather)	ηλιόλουστος	eeleeoloostos
sunrise	η ανατολή	ee anatolee
sunset	το ηλιοβασί-λεμα	to eeleeovasee lema
sunshade	η ομπρέλα	ee ombrela
supermarket	το σούπερ-μάρκετ	to supermarket
supper	το δείπνο	to dheepno
surfing	το σέρφινγκ	to serfeeng
surname	το επώνυμο	to eponeemo
to sweat	ιδρώνω	eedhrono
sweater	το πουλόβερ	to poolover
sweet (dessert)	το γλυκό	to ghleeko
to swim	κολυμπώ	koleembo

English	Greek	Pronunciation
swimming pool	η πισίνα	ee peeseena
swimsuit	το μαγιό	to mayo
to switch on	ανάβω	anavo
to switch off	σβήνω	sveeno
swollen (ankle, etc.)	πρησμένος	preesmenos
T		
table	το τραπέζι	to trapezee
tablet	το χάπι	to khapee
to take	παίρνω	perno
to take out (from bank account)	βγάζω	vghazo
	αποσύρω	aposeero
to talk	μιλώ	meelo
tall	ψηλός	pseelos
to taste	δοκιμάζω	dhokeemazo
taste noun	η γεύση	ee yefsee
taxi	το ταξί	to taksee
tea	το τσάι	to tsaee
to teach	διδάσκω	dheedhasko

English	Greek	pronunciation
teacher	ο δάσκαλος/ η δασκάλα	o dhaskalos/ o dhaskala
teeth	τα δόντια	ta dhondya
telephone	το τηλέφωνο	to teelefono
telephone call	το τηλεφώνημα	to telefoneema
television	η τηλεόραση	ee teeleorasee
to tell (story)	λέγω	legho
temperature	διηγούμαι	dhee-eeghoome
to have a temperature	η θερμοκρασία	ee thermokraseea
	έχω πυρετό	ekho peereto
temporary	προσωρινός	prosoreenos
tennis	το τένις	to tenes
tent	η σκηνή	ee skeenee
to text	στέλνω μήνυμα	stelno meeneema
I'll text you	θα σου στείλω μήνυμα	tha soo steelo meeneema
thank you	μήνυμα	meeneema
	ευχαριστώ	efkhareesto
that	εκείνος	ekeenos
that book	εκείνο το βιβλίο	ekeeno to veevleeo

English	Greek	pronunciation
that one	εκείνο	ekeeno
theatre	το θέατρο	to theatro
then	τότε	tote
there	εκεί	ekee
there is	υπάρχει	eeparkhee
there are	υπάρχουν	eeparkhoon
these (feminine)	αυτά/	afta/
(masculine)	αυτές/	aftee/
(neuter)	αυτά	aftes
these books	αυτά τα βιβλία	afta ta veevleea
they	αυτοί	aftee
thief	ο κλέφτης	o kleftes
thing	το πράγμα	to praghma
thirsty:	διψάω	dheepsao
I'm thirsty		
this (masculine)	αυτός/	aftos/
(feminine)	αυτή/	aftee/
(neuter)	αυτό	afto
this book	αυτό το βιβλίο	afto to veevleeo
this one	αυτό	afto

English – Greek

those	εκείνοι	ekeenee
those books	εκείνα τα βιβλία	ekeena ta veevleea
through	διαμέσου	dheeamesoo
ticket	το εισιτήριο	to eeseeteereeo
tie	η γραβάτα	ee ghravata
till (cash)	το ταμείο	to tameeo
till (until)	μέχρι	mekhree
time (by the clock)	η ώρα	ee ora
what time is it?	τι ώρα είναι;	tee ora eene?
timetable (buses, trains, etc) (school, shop opening hours etc)	το δρομολόγιο	to dromoloyeeo
	το ωράριο	to orareeo
tip (to waiter, etc)	το πουρμπουάρ	to poorbooar
tired	κουρασμένος	koorasmenos
tissue	το χαρτομάντηλο	to khartomandeelo

to	σε	se
	στο/	sto/
to the (masculine)	στη/	stee/
(feminine)	στο	sto
(neuter)		
to Greece	στην Ελλάδα	steen eladha
tobacco	ο καπνός	o kapnos
together	μαζί	mazee
toilet	η τουαλέτα	ee tooaleta
toilet paper	το χαρτί υγείας	to khartee eeyeeas
toll	τα διόδια	ta dheeodheea
tomato	η ντομάτα	ee domata
tomorrow	αύριο	avreeo
tonight	απόψε	apopse
too (also)	επίσης	epeeses
(too much)	πάρα πολύ	para polee
tooth	το δόντι	to dhondee
toothache	ο πονόδοντος	o ponodhondos
toothbrush	η οδοντόβουρ– τσα	ee odhonto- voortsa
toothpaste	η οδοντόκρεμα	ee odhondokrema

top (of mountain)	το πάνω μέρος	to pano meros	
total	η κορυφή	ee koreefee	
tour	το σύνολο	to seenolo	
tourist	η εκδρομή	ee ekdhromee	
	ο τουρίστας/	o tooreestas/	
tourist office	η τουρίστρια	ee tooreestreea	
	το τουριστικό	to tooreesteeko	
	γραφείο	ghrafeeo	
town	η πόλη	ee polee	
town centre	το κέντρο της	to kendro tees	
	πόλης	polees	
town plan	ο χάρτης της	o khartees tees	
	πόλης	polees	
toy	το παιχνίδι	to pekhneedhee	
traditional	παραδοσιακός	paradhoseeakos	
traffic	η κυκλοφορία	ee keekloforeea	
traffic lights	τα φανάρια	ta fanarya	
	(της τροχαίας)	(tees trokheas)	
train	το τρένο	to treno	
to translate	μεταφράζω	metafrazo	

to travel	ταξιδεύω	takseedhevo	
travel agent	ο ταξιδιωτικός	o takseedhyotee-	
	πράκτορας	kos praktoras	
travellers'	τα ταξιδιωτικά	ta takseedhyo-	
cheques	τσεκ	teeka tsek	
tree	το δέντρο	to dhendro	
trip	η εκδρομή	ee ekdhromee	
trousers	ο μπελάς	o belas	
true	το παντελόνι	to pandelonee	
to try	αληθινός	aleetheenos	
to try on	προσπαθώ	prospatho	
T-shirt	δοκιμάζω	dhokeemazo	
to turn	το μπλουζάκι	to bloozakee	
to turn off (on a journey)	στρίβω	streevo	
(radio, etc.)	στρίβω	streevo	
(engine, light)	κλείνω	kleeno	
	σβήνω	sveeno	

English – Greek

English – Greek

English	Greek	Pronunciation
to turn on (radio, TV) (engine, light)	ανοίγω ανάβω	aneegho anavo
TV	η τηλεόραση	ee teeleorasee
twice	δύο φορές	dheeo fores
twin-bedded	το δίκλινο δωμάτιο	to dheekleeno dhomateeo
U		
ugly	άσχημος	askheemos
umbrella	η ομπρέλα	ee ombrela
uncle	ο θείος	o theeos
uncomfortable	άβολος	avolos
under	κάτω από	kato apo
underground (railway)	το μετρό	to metro
to understand	καταλαβαίνω	kataleno
underwear	τα εσώρουχα	ta esorookha
unemployed	άνεργος	anerghos
United States	οι Ηνωμένες Πολιτείες	ee eenomenes poleeteeyes
university	το πανεπιστήμιο	to panepeesteemeeo
until	μέχρι/ έως	mekhree/ eos
upstairs	πάνω	pano
urgently	επειγόντως	epeeghondos
to use	χρησιμοποιώ	khreeseemopeeo
useful	χρήσιμος	khreeseemos
usually	συνήθως	seeneethos
V		
vacancy (room)	το διαθέσιμο δωμάτιο	to dheeatheseemo dhomateeo
valuable	πολύτιμος	poleeteemos
value	η αξία	ee akseea
VAT	ο ΦΠΑ	o fee pee a
vegetables	τα λαχανικά	ta lakhaneeka
vegetarian	ο χορτοφάγος	o khortofaghos

very	πολύ	polee
video	το βίντεο	to veedeo
view	η θέα	ee thea
villa	η βίλλα	ee veela
village	το χωριό	to khoryo
visa	η βίζα	ee veesa
to visit	επισκέπτομαι	epeeskeptome
visit	επίσκεψη	ee epeeskepsee
voice	η φωνή	ee fonee

W

to wait for	περιμένω	pereemeno
waiter	το γκαρσόνι	to garsonee
waiting room	η αίθουσα αναμονής	ee ethoosa anamonees
waitress	η σερβιτόρα	ee serveetora
Wales	η Ουαλία	ee oaleea
walk	ο περίπατος	o pereepatos
to walk	περπατώ	perpato
wall	ο τοίχος	o teekhos

wallet	το πορτοφόλι	to portofolee
to want	θέλω	thelo
warm	ζεστός	zestos
to wash (clothes)	πλένω	pleno
(oneself)	πλένομαι	plenome
watch noun	το ρολόι	to roloee
to watch (TV)	βλέπω	vlepo
(someone's luggage)	προσέχω	prosekho
water	το νερό	to nero
watermelon	το καρπούζι	to karpoozee
way (method)	ο τρόπος	o tropos
this way	από 'δω	apodho
that way	από 'κει	apokee
we	εμείς	emees
weak	αδύνατος	adheenatos
to wear	φορώ	foro
weather	ο καιρός	o keros
wedding	ο γάμος	o ghamos
week	η εβδομάδα	ee evdhomadha

English - Greek

weekend	το σαββατοκύ- ριακο	to savatokeeryako	
weekly (rate, etc.)	εβδομαδιαίος	evdhomadhee- eos	
weight	το βάρος	to varos	
welcome	καλώς ήλθατε	kalos eelthate	
well (healthy)	καλά	kala	
Welsh (person)	ο Ουαλός/ η Ουαλή	o ooalos/ ee ooalee	
west	η δύση	ee dheesee	
what	τι	tee	
what is it?	τι είναι;	tee eene?	
wheelchair	η αναπηρική καρέκλα	ee anapeerekee karekla	
when?	πότε;	pote?	
where?	πού;	poo?	
which? (masculine)	ποιος;	pyos?	
(feminine)	ποια;	pya?	
(neuter)	ποιο;	pyo?	
which is it?	ποιο είναι;	pyo eene?	

while	ενώ	eno	
white	άσπρος	aspros	
who?	ποιος;	pyos?	
whole	όλος	olos	
whose: whose is it?	ποιανού είναι;	pyanoo eene?	
why?	γιατί;	yatee?	
wide	πλατύς	plates	
wife	η σύζυγος	ee seezeeghos	
wind	ο αέρας	o a-eras	
window	το παράθυρο	to paratheero	
wine	το κρασί	to krasee	
winter	ο χειμώνας	o kheemonas	
with	με	me	
without	χωρίς	khorees	
woman	η γυναίκα	ee yeeneka	
word	η λέξη	ee leksee	
to work (person)	η δουλειά	ee dhoolya	
(machine)	δουλεύω λειτουργεί	dhoolevo leetoorghee	

worried	ανήσυχος	aneeseekhos
to write	γράφω	ghrafo
wrong	λάθος	lathos
you're wrong	κάνετε λάθος	kanete lathos

Y

year	ο χρόνος	o khronos
yellow	κίτρινος	keetreenos
yes	ναι	ne
yesterday	χτες	khtes
yet	ακόμα	akoma
not yet	όχι ακόμα	okhee akoma
yoghurt	το γιαούρτι	to yaoortee
you (singular/ plural)	εσύ/ εσείς	esee/ esees
young	νέος	neos
youth hostel	ο ξενώνας νεότητος	o ksenonas neoteetos

Z

| zero | το μηδέν | to meedhen |
| zone | η ζώνη | ee zonee |

Greek – English

αΑ

Greek	Pronunciation	English
άγαλμα (το)	aghalma	statue
αγάπη (η)	aghapee	love
αγαπώ	aghapo	to love
Αγγλία (η)	angleea	England
αγγλικός/ή/ό	angleekos/ee/o	English (thing)
Άγγλος/	anglos/	Englishman/
Αγγλίδα (ο/η)	angleedha	-woman
άγιος/ α/ο	agheeos/a/o	holy, saint
Άγιον Όρος (το)	agheeon oros	Mount Athos
αγορά (η)	aghora	market
αγοράζω	aghorazo	to buy
αγόρι (το)	aghoree	young boy
άδεια (η)	adheea	permit, licence
άδεια οδήγησης	adheea odheegheesees	driving licence
άδειος/ α/ο	adheeos/a/o	empty
αδελφή (η)	adhelfee	sister
αδελφός (ο)	adhelfos	brother
αδίκημα (το)	adheekeema	offence
αέρας (ο)	aeras	wind
αεροδρόμιο (το)	aerodromeeo	airport
αεροπλάνο (το)	aeroplano	aeroplane
αεροπορικό εισιτήριο (το)	aeroporeeko eeseeteereeo	air ticket
Αθήνα (η)	atheena	Athens
αθλητικό κέντρο (το)	athleeteeko kendro	sports centre
αθλητισμός (ο)	athleeteesmos	sports
Αιγαίο (το)	egheo	the Aegean Sea
αίμα (το)	ema	blood
αίτηση (η)	eteesee	application
ακούω	akoo-o	to hear
Ακρόπολη (η)	akropolee	the Acropolis
ακτή (η)	aktee	beach, shore
αλάτι (το)	alatee	salt
αλλαγή (η)	alaghee	change

αλλάζω / alazo / to change
αμάξι (το) / amaksee / car, vehicle
αμερικάνικος/ η/ο / amereekaneekos/ ee/o / American (thing)
Αμερικανός/ Αμερικανίδα / amereekanos/ amereekaneedha / American (man/woman)
Αμερική (η) / amereekee / America
αμέσως / amesos / at once, immediately
άμμος (η) / amos / sand
αν / an / if
ανάβω / anavo / to switch on
αίθουσα / ethoosa / waiting room
αναμονής / anamonees /
ανάπηρος/ η/ο / anapeeros/ee/o / handicapped, disabled
ανατολή (η) / anatolee / east, sunrise
ανατολικός/ η/ο / anatoleekos/ee/o / eastern

αναψυκτικό (το) / anapseekteeko / soft drink
άνδρας (ο) / andhras / man, male
ανθοπωλείο (το) / anthopoleeo / florist's
άνθρωπος (ο) / anthropos / person
ανοίγω / aneegho / to open
άνοιξη (η) / aneeksee / spring (season)
ανταλλαγή (η) / andalaghee / exchange
αντιβιοτικά (τα) / andeeveeoteeka / antibiotics
αντίγραφο (το) / andeeghrafo / copy
αντίκες (οι) / aneekes / antiques
αντίο / andeeo / goodbye
απαγορεύω / apaghorevo / to forbid: no...
απάντηση (η) / apanteesee / answer
απέναντι / apenantee / opposite
απογείωση (η) / apogheeosee / takeoff
απόγευμα (το) / apoyevma / afternoon
απόδειξη (η) / apodheeksee / receipt

Greek – English

Greek	Pronunciation	English
αποσκευές (οι)	aposkeves	luggage
αναζήτηση (η)	anazeeteesee	left-luggage (office)
αποσκευών	aposkevon	
απόψε	apope	tonight
αργότερα	arghotera	later
αρέσω	areso	to please
μου αρέσει	moo aresee	I like
δεν μου αρέσει	dhen moo aresee	I don't like
σου αρέσει	soo aresee	you like
δεν σου αρέσει	dhen soo aresee	you don't like
αριθμός (ο)	areethmos	number
αριθμός τηλεφώνου	areethmos teelefonoo	telephone number
αριστερά	areestera	left (opposite of right)
αρνί (το)	arnee	lamb
αρρώστια (η)	arosteea	illness
άρρωστος/η/ο	arostos/ee/o	ill
αρχαίος/α/ο	arkheos/a/o	ancient
αρχή (η)	arkhee	start, beginning
αρχίζω	arkheezo	to begin, to start
άρωμα (το)	aroma	perfume
ασανσέρ (το)	asanser	lift, elevator
ασθενής (ο/η)	asthenees	patient
ασπιρίνη (η)	aspeereenee	aspirin
άσπρος/η/ο	aspros/ee/o	white
αστυνομία (η)	asteenomeea	police
αστυνομία	asteenomeea	immigration
αλλοδαπών	alodhapon	police
αστυνομία	eleeneekee	Greek police
Ελληνική		
αστυνομικό	asteenomeeko	police station
τμήμα (το)	tmeema	
αστυνομικός	asteenomeekos	police station
σταθμός (ο)	stathmos	
αστυνόμος (ο)	asteenomos	policeman
ασφάλεια (η)	asfalea	insurance, fuse
ιατρική	eeatreekee	medical
ασφάλιση	asfaleesee	insurance
άτομο (το)	atomo	person

ατύχημα (το)	ateekheema	accident
αυτοκίνητο (το)	aftokeeneeto	car
ενοικιάσεις αυτοκινήτων	eneekyasees aftokeeneeton	car hire
συνεργείο αυτοκινήτων	seenergheeon aftokeeneeton	car repairs
αυτοκινητό-δρομος (ο)	aftokeeneeto-dhromos	motorway
αυτόματος/η/ο	aftomatos/ee/o	automatic
άφιξη (η)	afeeksee	arrival

ßΒ

βαγόνι (το)	vaghonee	carriage (train)
βάζω	vazo	to put
βαλίτσα (η)	valeetsa	suitcase
βαρέλι μπύρα από βαρέλι	beera apo varelee	draught beer

βαρελίσιο κρασί (το)	vareeleeseo krasee	house wine
βάρκα (η)	varka	boat
βάρος (το)	varos	weight
βγάζω	vghazo	to take off
βγαίνω	vgheno	to go out
βενζίνη (η)	venzenee	petrol, gasoline
βήχας (ο)	veekhas	cough
βιβλίο (το)	veevleeo	book
βιβλιοπωλείο (το)	veevleeopoleeo	bookshop
βλέπω	vlepo	to see
βοήθεια (η)	voetheea	help
οδική βοήθεια	odheekee voeetheea	breakdown service
πρώτες βοήθειες	protes voeethee-es	casualty (hospital)
βόλτα (η)	volta	walk, drive, trip
βόρειος/α/ο	voreeos/a/o	northern
βορράς (ο)	voras	north

Greek - English

Greek	Pronunciation	English
βουνό (το)	voono	mountain
Βράδυ (το)	vradhee	evening
βραδινό (το)	vradheeno	evening meal
βράζω	vrazo	to boil
Βρετανία (η)	vretaneea	Britain
Βρετανός/ Βρετανίδα (ο/η)	vretanos/ vretaneedha	British (man/woman)
βρίσκω	vreesko	to find
βρόμικος/η/ο	vromeekos/ee/o	dirty
βροχή (η)	vrokhee	rain

ΥΓ

Greek	Pronunciation	English
Γάλα (το)	ghala	milk
γαλάζιος/α/ο	ghalazeeos/a/o	blue, light blue
γάμος (ο)	ghamos	wedding, marriage
γειά σας	ya sas	hello, goodbye (formal)
γειά σου	ya soo	hello, goodbye (informal)
γεμάτος/η/ο	yematos/ee/o	full
γενέθλια (τα)	yenethleea	birthday
γενικός/ή/ό	yeneekos/ee/o	general
γέννηση (η)	yeneesee	birth
γεύμα (το)	yevma	meal
γέφυρα (η)	yefeera	bridge
για	ya	for
γιαγιά (η)	yaya	grandmother
γιατί;	yatee?	why?
γιατρός (ο/η)	yatros	doctor
γιορτή (η)	yortee	festival, celebration, name day
γιος (ο)	yos	son
γκάζι (το)	gazee	accelerator (car), gas
γκαλερί	galeree	art gallery, art sales

γκαράζ (το)	garaz	garage
γκαρσόν (το)/ γκαρσόνι (το)/ ο	garson/garsone	waiter
γλυκός/ιά/ό	ghleekos/ya/o	sweet
Γλυκό (το)/ Γλυκά (τα)	ghleeko/ghleeka	cakes and pastries, desserts
Γλυπτική (η)	ghleepteekee	sculpture
Γλώσσα (η)	ghlosa	tongue, language, sole (fish)
γονείς (οι)	ghonees	parents
γράμμα (το)	ghrama	letter
γράμμα κατεπείγον	ghrama katepeeghon	express letter
γράμμα συστημένο	ghrama seesteemeno	recorded delivery
γραμμάριο (το)	ghramareeo	gram
Γραμματοκιβώτιο (το)	ghramatokeevo-teeo	letter box

γραμματό-σημο (το)	ghramatoseemo	stamp
Γραφείο (το)	ghrafeeo	office, desk
Γραφείο Τουρισμού	ghrafeeo tooreesmoo	Tourist Office
Γράφω	ghrafo	to write
γρήγορα	ghreegora	quickly
γρίπη (η)	ghreepee	influenza
γυαλί (το)	yalee	glass
γυαλιά (τα)	yalya	glasses
γυαλιά ηλίου	yalya eeleeoo	sunglasses
γυμναστήριο (το)	yeemnasteereeo	gym
γυναίκα (η)	yeeneka	woman
γύρω	yeero	round, about
γωνία (η)	ghoneea	corner

δΔ

| δάσος (το) | dhasos | forest, wood |
| δείπνο (το) | dheepno | dinner |

Greek – English

Greek - English

Greek	Transliteration	English
δέκα	dheka	ten
Δελφοί (οι)	dhelfee	Delphi
δεν	dhen	not
δεξιά	dhekseea	right (opposite of left)
δέρμα (το)	dherma	skin, leather
δεσποινίς/ δεσποινίδα (η)	dhespeenees/ dhespeeneedha	Miss
δεύτερος/η/ο	dhefteros/ee/o	second
δήλωση (η)	dheelosee	announcement
είδη προς δήλωση	eedhe pros dheelosee	goods to declare
ουδέν προς δήλωση	oodhen pros dheelosee	nothing to declare
δημαρχείο (το)	dheemarkheeo	town hall
δημόσιος/α/ο	dheemoseeos	public/state
δημόσια έργα	dheemoseea ergha	road works
δημόσιος κήπος	dheemoseeos keepos	public gardens
δημοτικός/ή/ό Δημοτική Αγορά	deemoteekos dheemoteekee aghora	public/municipal public market
διάβαση (η)	dheeavasee	crossing
διαβατήριο (το)	dheeavateereeo	passport
διαβήτης (ο)	dheeaveetees	diabetes
διαδρομή (η)	dheeadhromee	route
διακεκριμένη θέση	dheeakekree- menee thesee	business class
διακοπές (οι)	dheeakopes	holidays
διάλειμμα (το)	dheealeema	interval, break
διαμέρισμα (το)	dheeamereesma	flat, apartment
διανυχτερεύει	dheeaneekhtereevee	open all night
διασκέδαση	dheeaskedhasee	entertainment
κέντρο διασ- κεδάσεως	kendro dheeas- kedhaseos	nightclub
διασταύρωση (η)	dheeastavrosee	crossroads, junction

Greek	Transliteration	English
διεθνής/ής/ές	dhee-ethnees/ees/es	international
διεύθυνση (η)	dhee-eftheensee	address
διευθυντής (ο)	dhee-eftheentees	manager
δικαστήριο (το)	dheekasteereeo	court
δικηγόρος (ο/η)	dheekeeghoros	lawyer
δίνω	dheeno	to give
διπλά	dheepla	next to
διπλός/ή/ό	dheeplos/ee/o	double
διπλό δωμάτιο	dheeplo domateeo	double room
διπλό κρεβάτι	dheeplo krevatee	double bed
δολάριο (το)	dholareeo	dollar
δόντι (το)	dhondee	tooth
δρομολόγιο (το)	dhromologheeo	timetable, route
δρόμος (ο)	dhromos	street, way
δύση (η)	dheesee	west, sunset
δύσκολος/η/ο	dheeskolos/ee/o	difficult
δυστύχημα (το)	dheesteekheema	accident, mishap
δυτικός/ή/ό	dheeteekos/ee/o	western
Δωδεκάνησος (τα)	dhodhekaneesa	the Dodecanese
δωμάτιο (το)	dhomateeo	room
δωρεάν	dhorean	free of charge
δώρο (το)	dhoro	present, gift

ε Ε

Greek	Transliteration	English
εβδομάδα (η)	evdhomadha	week
εγγύηση (η)	engheeyeesee	guarantee
εδώ	edho	here
εθνικός/ή/ό	ethneekos/ee/o	national
Εθνικό Θέατρο	ethneeko theatro	National Theatre
εθνική οδός	ethneekee odhos	motorway
έθνος (το)	ethnos	nation
εθνικότητα	ethneekoteeta	nationality
ειδικός/ή/ό	eedheekos/ee/o	special, specialist
είδος (το)	eedhos	kind, sort
είδη	eedhee	goods

Greek – English

Greek	Transliteration	English
είμαι	eeme	to be
εισιτήριο (το)	eeseeteereeo	ticket
εκδόσεις εισιτηρίων	ekdhosees eeseeteereeon	ticket office
εκεί	ekee	there
έκθεση (η)	ekthese	exhibition
εκκλησία (η)	ekleeseea	church, chapel
έκπτωση (η)	ekptosee	discount
εκτελούνται έργα	ekteloonde ergha	road works
εκτός	ektos	except, unless
εκτός Λειτουργίας	ektos leetoorgheeas	out of order
Έλα!	ela!	come on! (singular)
Ελάτε!	elate!	come on! (plural)
ελαιόλαδο (το)	eleoladho	olive oil
ελαττώνω	elatono	to reduce, to decrease
ελαττώσατε ταχύτητα	elatosate takheeteeta	reduce speed
έλεγχος (ο)	elenkhos	control
έλεγχος διαβατηρίων	elenkhos dheeavateereeon	passport control
έλεγχος εισιτηρίων	elenkhos eeseeteereeon	check-in
ελεύθερος/η/ο	eleftheros/ee/o	single, free
ελιά (η)	elya	olive, olive tree
Ελλάδα (η)	eladha	Greece
Έλληνας/ Ελληνίδα (ο/η)	eleenas/ eleeneedha	Greek (man/woman)
ελληνικά (τα)	eleeneeka	Greek (language)
ελληνικός/ή/ό	eleeneekos/ee/o	Greek (thing)
εμπρός	embros	forward, in front, 'hello!' (on phone)
ένας/μία/ένα	enas/meea/ena	one
ενήλικος (ο)	eneeleekos	adult

Greek	Transliteration	English
εννέα / εννιά	enea/enya	nine
ενοικιάζω	eneekeeazo	to rent, to hire
ενοικιάζεται	eneekeeazete	to let
ενοικιάζεσες	eneekeeasees	for hire
ενοίκιο (το)	eneekeeo	rent
εντάξει	endaksee	all right, OK
έντυπο (το)	endeepo	form (to fill in)
έξι	eksee	six
εξυπηρέτηση (η)	ekseepereeteesee	service
έξω	ekso	out, outside
εξωτερικός: το εξωτερικό	ekso: to eksotereeko	abroad
ΕΟΤ	e-ot	Greek Tourist Organisation
επάγγελμα (το)	epanghelma	occupation, profession
επείγον/ επείγουσα	epeeghon/ epeeghoosa	urgent, express
επείγοντα	epeeghonta	casualty
περιστατικά	perestateeka	department
επιβάτης/ τρια (ο/η)	epeevatees/treea	passenger
επιβεβαιώνω	epeeveveono	to confirm
επιβεβαιώσε	epeevevasee	boarding
κάρτα	karta	boarding card
επιβεβαιώσεως	epeeveevaseos	
επειδή	epeedhee	because
επιδόρπιο (το)	epeedhorpeeo	dessert
επικίνδυνος/ η/ο	epeekeendeenos/ ee/o	dangerous
επίσης	epeeses	also, the same to you
επισκέπτης (ο)	epeeskeptees	visitor
επίσκεψη (η)	epeeskepsee	visit
επιστροφή (η)	epeestrofee	return, return ticket
επιστροφές	epeestrofes	returned goods, refunds
επιταγή (η)	epeetaghee	cheque, invoice

Greek – English

Greek	Pronunciation	English
επόμενος/η/ο	epomenos/ee/o	next
εποχή (η)	epokhee	season
επτά / εφτά	epta/efta	seven
Επτάνησα (τα)	eptaneesa	Ionian Islands
επώνυμο (το)	eponeemo	surname, last name
έργα (τα)	ergha	works
έργο	ergo	film, play, TV program
εργοστάσιο (το)	erghostaseeo	factory
έρχομαι	erkhome	to come
ερώτηση (η)	erotesee	question
εστιατόριο (το)	esteeatoreeo	restaurant
εσώρουχα (τα)	esorookha	underwear, lingerie
εσωτερικός πτήσεις εσωτερικού	pteesees esotereekoo	domestic flights
έτος (το)	etos	year
έτσι	etsee	so, like this
ευθεία (η)	eftheea	straight
ευθύνη (η)	eftheenee	responsibility
ευκαιρία (η)	efkereea	opportunity, bargain
εύκολος/η/ο	efkolos/ee/o	easy
Ευρωπαϊκή Ένωση	evropaeekee enosee	European Union
ευρωπαϊκός/ή/ό	evropaeekos/ee/o	European
Ευρώπη (η)	evropee	Europe
ευχαριστώ	efkhareesto	thank you
εφημερίδα (η)	efeemereedha	newspaper
έχω	ekho	to have

ΖZ

Greek	Pronunciation	English
ζάλη (η)	zalee	dizziness
ζαμπόν (το)	zambon	ham
ζάχαρη (η)	zakharee	sugar

ζαχαρο-πλαστείο (το)	zakharoplasteo	patisserie
ζέστη (η)	zestee	heat
κάνει ζέστη	kanee zestee	it's hot
ζευγάρι (το)	zevgharee	couple
ζημιά (η)	zeemya	damage
ζητώ	zeeto	to ask, to seek
ζυμαρικά (τα)	zeemareekha	pasta products
ζωγραφιά (η)	zoghrafya	picture, painting
ζώνη (η)	zonee	belt
ζώνη ασφαλείας	zonee asfaleeas	safety belt, seat belt
ζώο (το)	zo-o	animal

ηΗ

η	ee	the (with feminine nouns)
ή	ee	or
ηλεκτρικός/ή/ό	eelektreekos/ee/o	electrical
ηλεκτρισμός (ο)	eelektresmos	electricity
ηλεκτρονικός/ή/ό	eelektroneekos/ee/o	electronic
ηλίαση (η)	eeleasee	sunstroke
ηλικία (η)	eelekeea	age
ηλιοβασίλεμα (το)	eeleeovaseelema	sunset
ηλιοθεραπεία (η)	eeleeotherapeea	sunbathing
ήλιος (ο)	eeleeos	sun
ημέρα (η)	eemera	day
ημερήσιος/α/ο	eemereeseeos/a/o	daily
ημερομηνία Λήξης	eemeromeeneea leekses	expiry date
ημιδιατροφή (η)	eemeedheeatrofee	half board
Ηνωμένο Βασίλειο (το)	eenomeno vaseeleeo	United Kingdom (UK)

Greek – English

Greek - English

Ηνωμένες Πολιτείες της Αμερικής (η)	eenomenes poleetee-es tees amereekees	United States of America	
ΗΠΑ		USA	
ησυχία (η)	eesekheea	calm, quiet	
Θ θ			
θάλασσα (η)	thalasa	sea	
θαλάσσιο σκι	thalaseeo skee	water-skiing	
θέατρο (το)	theatro	theatre	
θέλω	thelo	to want	
θεός/θεά (ο/η)	theos/thea	god/goddess	
θεραπεία (η)	therapeea	treatment	
θέρμανση (η)	thermansee	heating	
θέση (η)	thesee	place, seat	
κράτηση θέσης	krateesee thesees	seat reservation	
οικονομική θέση	eekonomeekee thesee	economy class	
πρώτη θέση	protee thesee	first class	

Θεσσαλονίκη (η)	thesaloneekee	Salonica/ Thessaloniki	
θύρα (η)	theera	gate (airport)	
θυρίδα (η)	theereedha	ticket window	
Ι ι			
ιατρική περίθαλψη (η)	eeatreekee pereethalpsee	medical treatment	
ιατρός (ο/η)	yatros	doctor	
ιδιοκτήτης/ τρια (ο/η)	eedheeokteetees/ treea	owner	
ιντερνετ (το)	eenternet	internet	
Ιόνιο Πέλαγος (το)	eoneeo pelaghos	Ionian sea	
ιπτάμενο δελφίνι	eeptameno dhelfeenee	hydrofoil (flying dolphin)	
Ισθμός της Κορίνθου	eesthmos tees koreenthoo	Corinth Canal	
ισοτιμία (η)	eesoteemeea	exchange rate	

ιστιοπλοΐα (η) — eesteeoploeea — sailing
ιχθυοπωλείο (το) — eekhtheeopoleeo — fishmonger's

kK

κάβα (η) — kava — wine merchant, off-licence
καζίνο (το) — kazeeno — casino
καθαριστήριο (το) — kathareesteereeo — dry-cleaner's
καθαρός/ή/ό — katharos/ee/o — clean
κάθε — kathe — every, each
κάθε μέρα — kathe mera — every day
καθημερινός/ή/ό — katheemereenos/ee/o — every day/daily
κάθισμα (το) — katheesma — seat
καθυστέρηση (η) — katheesteresee — delay
και — ke — and
καιρός (ο) — keros — weather, time

κακός/ή/ό — kakos/ee/o — bad
καλά — kala — well, all right
καλημέρα — kaleemera — good morning
καληνύχτα — kaleeneekhta — good night
καλησπέρα — kaleespera — good evening
καλοκαίρι (το) — kalokeree — summer
καλοριφέρ (το) — kaloreefer — central heating, radiator
καλοψημένο — kalopseemeno — well done (meat)
καμπίνα (η) — kambeena — cabin
κανάλι (το) — kanalee — canal, channel (TV)
κανένας — kanenas — no-one
καντίνα (η) — kanteena — mobile roadside cafe
κάνω — kano — to do
καπέλο (το) — kapelo — hat
καπνίζω — kapneezo — to smoke
καράβι (το) — karavee — boat, ship

Greek – English

κάρβουνο (το)	karvoono	coal, charcoal
στα κάρβουναν	sta karvoona	charcoal-grilled
καρδιά (η)	kardheea	heart
καρναβάλι (το)	karnavalee	carnival
καροτσάκι (το)	karotsakee	pushchair
καροτσάκι αναπηρικό	karotsakee anapeereeko	wheelchair
κάρτα (η)	karta	card, postcard
κάρτα επιβιβάσεως	karta epeeveevaseos	boarding card
πιστωτική κάρτα	peestoteekee karta	credit card
καρτοτηλέφωνο	kartoteelefono	card phone
καρτποστάλ (το)	kartpostal	postcard
κάστρο (το)	kastro	castle, fortress
καταιγίδα (η)	kategheedha	storm

καταλαβαίνω	katalaveno	to understand
καταλαβαίνεις; (familiar form)	katalavenees?	do you understand?
καταλαβαίνετε; (polite form)	katalavenete?	do you understand?
κατάλογος (ο)	kataloghos	list, menu, directory
κατασκήνωση (η)	kataskeenosee	camping
κατάστημα (το)	katasteema	shop
κατεπείγον/κατεπείγουσα	katepeeghon/katepeeghoosa	urgent, express
κατηγορία (η)	kateeghoreea	class (of hotel)
κατσίκα (η)	katseeka	goat
κάτω	kato	under, lower, down
καύσιμα (τα)	kafseema	fuel
καφέ	kafe	brown

καφενείο (το)	kafeneeo	coffee house	κερνώ	kerno	to buy a drink
καφές (ο)	kafes	coffee (usually Greek)	να κεράσω	na keraso	can I buy (you) a drink...?
καφές γλυκός	kafes ghleekos	sweet coffee	κεφάλι (το)	kefalee	head
καφές μέτριος	kafes metreeos	medium sweet coffee	κεφτέδες (οι)	keftedhes	meatballs
καφές σκέτος	kafes sketos	strong black coffee	κήπος (ο)	keepos	garden
καφές φραπέ	kafes frape	iced coffee (Nescafé®)	κιβώτιο (το)	keevoteeo	large box
			κιλό (το)	keelo	kilo
καφετέρια (η)	kafetereea	cafeteria	κίνδυνος (ο)	keendheenos	danger
κεντρικός/ή/ό	kendreekos/ee/o	central	κινητό (το)	keeneeto	mobile phone
κέντρο (το)	kendro	centre	κίτρινος/η/ο	keetreenos/ee/o	yellow
κέντρο δια-σκεδάσεως	kendro dheeas-kedhaseos	nightclub	κλείνω	kleeno	to close
			κλέφτης (ο)	kleftees	thief
κέντρο υγείας αθλητικό	kendro eegheeas athleeteeko	health centre	κλινική (η)	kleeneekee	clinic, hospital, ward
κέντρο	kendro	sports centre	κοιμάμαι	keemame	to sleep
Κέρκυρα (η)	kerkeera	Corfu	κόκκινος/η/ο	kokeenos/ee/o	red
κέρμα (το)	kerma	coin	κολοκυθάκι (το)	kolokeethakee	courgette
			κολύμπι (το)	koleembee	swimming

Greek – English

Greek – English

κολυμπώ	koleembo	to swim	κουτί (το)	kootee	box
κομμωτήριο (το)	komoteereeo	hairdresser's	κρασί (το)	krasee	wine
κομπιούτερ (το)	kompyooter	computer	κράτηση (η)	krateesee	reservation
			κράτηση θέσης	krateesee theses	seat reservation
κοντά	konda	near	κρέας (το)	kreas	meat
κόρη (η)	koree	daughter	κρέας αρνίσιο	kreas arneesyo	lamb
κορίτσι (το)	koreetsee	young girl	κρέας	kreas	
κοσμήματα (τα)	kosmeemata	jewellery	μοσχαρίσιο	moskhareesyo	beef
			κρέας χοιρινό	kreas kheereeno	pork
κοστούμι (το)	kostoomee	man's suit	κρεβάτι (το)	krevatee	bed
κότα (η)	kota	hen	κρεβατοκά–	krevatokama-	bedroom
κουβέρ (το)	koover	cover-charge	μαρα (η)	mara	
κουβέρτα (η)	kooverta	blanket, cover	κρέμα (η)	krema	cream
κουζίνα (η)	koozeena	kitchen, cuisine	κρεμμύδι (το)	kremeedhee	onion
ελληνική	eleeneekee	Greek cuisine	κρεοπωλείο	kreopoleeo	butcher's shop
κουζίνα	koozeena		(το)		
κουνούπι (το)	koonoopee	mosquito	Κρήτη (η)	kreetee	Crete
κουρείο (το)	kooreeo	barber's shop	κρουαζιέρα (η)	krooazyera	cruise
κουτάλι (το)	kootalee	spoon	κρύος/α/ο	kreeos/a/o	cold

κυβέρνηση (η)	keeverneesee	government	
Κυκλάδες (οι)	keekladhes	Cyclades (islands)	
κύκλος (ο)	keeklos	circle	
κυκλοφορία (η)	keekloforea	traffic, circulation	
κυλικείο (το)	keeleekeeo	canteen, cafeteria	
Κύπρος (η)	keepros	Cyprus	
Κύπριος/	keepreeos/	from Cyprus,	
Κυπρία (ο/η)	keepreea	Cypriot (man/woman)	
κυρία (η)	keereea	Mrs, lady	
κύριος (ο)	keereeos	Mr, gentleman	
κωδικός (ο)	kodheekos	code	
κωμωδία (η)	komodheea	comedy	

ΛΛ

λάδι (το)	ladhee	oil	
λάδι ελιάς	ladhee elyas	olive oil	
λαϊκός/ή/ό	laeekos/ee/o	popular, folk	
λαϊκή αγορά	laeekee aghora	market	
λαϊκή τέχνη	laeekee tekhnee	folk art	
λαχανικά (τα)	lakhaneeka	vegetables	
λεμονάδα (η)	lemonadha	lemonade	
λεμόνι (το)	lemonee	lemon	
λεξικό (το)	lekseeko	dictionary	
λεπτό (το)	lepto	minute	
λεπτός/ή/ό	leptos/ee/o	thin, slim	
λευκός/ή/ό	lefkos/ee/o	white	
λεφτά (τα)	lefta	money	
λέω	leo	to say	
λεωφορείο (το)	leoforeeo	bus	
λήξη (η)	leeksee	expiry	
λίγος/η/ο	leeghos/ee/o	a few, a little	
λιμάνι (το)	leemanee	port, harbour	
Λιμενικό	leemeneeko	coastguard,	
Σώμα (το)	soma	Port Police	
λίμνη (η)	leemnee	lake	
λίρα (η)	leera	pound	

Greek – English

Greek – English

Greek	Pronunciation	English
λίτρο (το)	leetro	litre
λογαριασμός (ο)	logharyasmos	bill
λουκάνικο (το)	lookaneeko	sausage
λουλούδι (το)	looloodhee	flower

μΜ

μαγαζί (το)	maghazee	shop
μαγειρεύω	magheerevo	to cook
μαγιό (το)	mayo	swimsuit
μακαρόνια (τα)	makaronya	spaghetti, pasta
μάλιστα	maleesta	yes, of course
μαλλί (το)	malee	wool
μαλλιά (τα)	malya	hair
μάλλινος/η/ο	maleenos/ee/o	woollen
μαμά (η)	mama	mum
μαντήλι (το)	mandeelee	handkerchief
μαξιλάρι (το)	makseelaree	pillow, cushion
μαργαρίνη (η)	marghareenee	margarine

Greek	Pronunciation	English
μάρμαρο (το)	marmaro	marble
μαρμελάδα (η)	marmeladha	jam
μαρούλι (το)	maroolee	lettuce
μαύρος/η/ο	mavros/ee/o	black
μαχαίρι (το)	makheree	knife
μαχαιροπήρουνα (τα)	makheeropeeroona	cutlery
με	me	with
μεγάλος/η/ο	meghalos	large, big
μέγαρο (το)	megharo	hall, palace, apartment block
μέγαρο μουσικής	megharo mooseekees	concert hall
μέγεθος (το)	megheethos	size
μέλι (το)	melee	honey
μενού (το)	menoo	menu
μέρα (η)	mera	day
μερίδα (η)	mereedha	portion
μέσα	mesa	in, inside
μεσάνυχτα (τα)	mesaneekhta	midnight

Greek	Pronunciation	English
μεσημέρι (το)	meseemeree	midday
μεσημεριανό (το)	meseemeryano	midday meal
Μεσόγειος (η)	mesoyeeos	Mediterranean Sea
μετά	meta	after
μεταξύ	metaksee	between, among
μεταφράζω	metafrazo	to translate
μετεωρο- λογικό δελτίο (το)	meteorologheeko dhelteeo	weather forecast
μετρητά (τα)	metreeta	cash
μετρό (το)	metro	underground (railway)
μηδέν	medhen	zero
μήλο (ο)	meelo	apple
μήνας (ο)	meenas	month
μήνας του μέλιτος	meenas too meleetos	honeymoon
μητέρα (η)	meetera	mother
μηχανάκι (το)	meekhanakee	moped, motorbike
μικρός/η/ό	meekros/ee/o	small
μιλάω/μιλώ	meelao/meelo	to speak
μολύβι (το)	moleevee	pencil
μόλυνση (η)	moleensee	infection, pollution
μοναστήρι (το)	monasteeree	monastery
μονόδρομος (ο)	monodhromos	one-way street
μονοπάτι (το)	monopatee	path
μόνος/η/ο	monos/ee/o	alone, only
μόνο είσοδος/ έξοδος	mono eesodhos/ eksodhos	entrance/ exit only
μοτοσυκλέτα (η)	motoseekleta	motorcycle
μουσείο (το)	mooseeo	museum
μουσική (η)	mooseekee	music
μπακάλης (ο)	bakalees	grocer
μπαμπάς (ο)	babas	dad
μπάνιο (το)	banyo	bathroom, bath

Greek – English

Greek – English

μπαταρία (η)	batareea	battery	νερό (το)	nero	water
μπιζέλια (τα)	beezelya	peas	νες, νεσκαφέ (το)	nes, neskafe	instant coffee
μπισκότο (το)	beeskoto	biscuit			
μπλε	ble	blue	νεφρό (το)	nefro	kidney
μπλούζα (η)	blooza	jumper	νησί (το)	neesee	island
μπουκάλι (το)	bookalee	bottle	νοίκι (το)	neeke	rent
μπριζόλα (η)	breezola	chop, steak	νομίζω	nomeezo	to think
μπύρα (η)	beera	beer	νόμισμα (το)	nomeesma	coin, currency
Μυκήνες	meekeenes	Mycenae	νοσοκομείο (το)	nosokomeeo	hospital
μύτη (η)	metee	nose			
μωρό (το)	moro	baby	νοσοκόμος/α (ο/η)	nosokomos/a	nurse

νN

ναι	ne	yes	νότος (ο)	notos	south
ναός (ο)	naos	temple, church	νούμερο (το)	noomero	number
ναυτία (η)	naftea	travel sickness	ντους (το)	doos	shower
νεκροταφείο (το)	nekrotafeeo	cemetery	νυκτερινός/ή/ό	neektereenos/ee/o	all-night (chemists, etc)
νεοελληνικά (τα)	neoeleeneeka	Modern Greek	νύχτα (η)	neekhta	night

Ξξ

Greek	Pronunciation	English
ξεκουράζω	ksekoorazo	to have a rest, to relax
ξεναγός (ο/η)	ksenaghos	guide
ξενοδοχείο (το)	ksenodhokheeo	hotel
ξένος/η/ο	ksenos/ee/o	foreign
ξέρω	ksero	to know
ξεχνώ	ksekhno	to forget
ξηρός/ή/ό	kseeros/ee/o	dry
ξύλο (το)	kseelo	wood

Οο

οδηγός (ο)	odheeghos	driver, guidebook
οδηγώ	odheegho	to drive
οδική βοήθεια (η)	odheekee voeetheea	breakdown service
οδοντιατρείο (το)	odhondeeatreeo	dental surgery
οδοντίατρος (ο/η)	odhondeeatros	dentist
οδοντόβουρτσα (η)	odhondovoortsa	toothbrush
οδοντόκρεμα (η)	odhondokrema	toothpaste
οδός (η)	odhos	road, street
οικογένεια (η)	eekoyeneea	family
οινοπνευματώδη ποτά (τα)	eenopnevmatodhee pota	spirits
οκτώ/οχτώ	okto/okhto	eight
Ολυμπία (η)	oleempeea	Olympia
ολυμπιακός/ή/ό	oleempeeakos/ee/o	Olympic
Όλυμπος (ο)	oleempos	Mount Olympus
ναυτικός όμιλος (ο)	nafteekos omeelos	sailing club
όμιλος (ο)	omeelos	club
ομπρέλα (η)	ombrela	umbrella
όνομα (το)	onoma	name

Greek – English

Greek - English

ονοματεπώνυμο (το)	onomateponeemo	full name
οργανωμένος/η/ο	orghanomenos/ee/o	organised
όρεξη: καλή όρεξη	kalee oreksee	enjoy your meal!
ορθόδοξος/η/ο	orthodhoksos/ee/o	orthodox
όροι ενοικιάσεως	oree eneekeeaseos	conditions of hire
ΟΣΕ	ose	Greek Railways
ΟΤΕ	ote	Greek Telecom
ούζο (το)	oozo	ouzo
όχι	okhee	no
πΠ		
παιδάκι (το)	paeedhakee	lamb chop
πάγος (ο)	paghos	ice
παίρνω	perno	to take
παγωμένος/η/ο	paghomenos/ee/o	frozen
παγωτό (το)	paghoto	ice cream
παιδικός/η/ο	pedheekos/ee/o	for children
παιδικά	pedheeka	children's wear
παιδικός σταθμός	pedheekos stathmos	crèche
πακέτο (το)	paketo	parcel, packet
Παναγία (η)	panagheea	the Virgin Mary
πανεπιστήμιο (το)	panepeesteemeeo	university
πανηγύρι (το)	panee-yeeree	festival
πάντα/πάντοτε	panda/pandote	always
παντελόνι (το)	pandelonee	trousers
παντοπωλείο (το)	pandopoleeo	grocer's
παντρεμένος/η/ο	pantremenos/ee/o	married
πάνω	pano	up, on, above

παπάς (o)	papas	priest
πάπλωμα (το)	paploma	duvet
παππούς (o)	papoos	grandfather
παπούτσι (το)	papootsee	shoe
παραγγέλνω	paranghelno	to order
παραγωγή: Ελληνικής παραγωγής	eleeneekees paraghoghees	produce of Greece
παράθυρο (το)	paratheero	window
παρακαλώ	parakalo	please
παραλία (η)	paralea	seashore, beach
παράσταση (η)	parastasee	performance
παρέα (η)	parea	company, group
Παρθενώνας (o)	parthenonas	the Parthenon
πάρκο (το)	parko	park
Πάσχα (το)	paskha	Easter
πατάτα (η)	patata	potato
πατέρας (o)	pateras	father

παυσίπονο (το)	pafseepono	painkiller
πάω	pao	to go
πεζόδρομο (το)	pezodhromeeo	pavement
πεθαμένος/η/ο	pethamenos/ee/o	dead
Πειραιάς (o)	peereas	Piraeus
πελάτης/πελάτισσα (o/η)	pelates/pelateesa	customer
Πελοπόννησος (η)	peloponeesos	Peloponnese
περιοδικό (το)	pereeodheeko	magazine
περιοχή (η)	pereeokhee	area
περίπατος n (o)	pereepatos	walk
περίπτερο (το)	pereeptero	kiosk
πετρέλαιο (το)	petreleo	diesel fuel
πετσέτα (η)	petseta	towel

Greek - English

πηγαίνω	peegheno	to go
πιάτο (το)	pyato	plate, dish
πίεση αίματος	peeyesee ematos	blood pressure
πινακοθήκη (η)	peenakotheekee	art gallery
πίνω	peeno	to drink
πιπέρι (το)	peeperee	ground pepper
πιπεριά (η)	peeperya	pepper (vegetable)
πισίνα (η)	peeseena	swimming pool
πιστοποιητικό (το)	peestopyeeteeko	certificate
πιστωτική κάρτα (η)	peestoteekee karta	credit card
πίσω	peeso	behind, back
πιτζάμα (η)	peezama	pyjamas
πιτσαρία (η)	peetsarea	pizzeria
πλαζ (η)	plaz	beach
πλάι	plaee	next to
πλατεία (η)	platea	square
πληροφορίες δρομολογίων (n)	pleeroforeeyes dhromologheeon	travel information
πληρωμή (n)	pleeromee	payment
πληρώνω	pleerono	to pay
πλοίο (το)	pleeo	ship
πλυντήριο (το)	pleenteereeo	washing machine
ποδήλατο (το)	podheelato	bicycle
ποδήλατο της θάλασσας	podheelato tis thalasas	pedalo
πόδι (το)	podhee	foot, leg
ποδόσφαιρο (το)	podhosfero	football
ποιος/ποια/ποιο	pyos/pya/pyo	who, which
ποιότητα (n)	peeoteeta	quality
πόλη (n)	polee	town, city
πολυκατάστημα (το)	poleekatasteema	department store

πολύς/πολλή/	polees/polee/	much, many
πολύ	polee	
πονόδοντος (ο)	ponodhontos	toothache
πονοκέφαλος (ο)	ponokefalos	headache
πόνος (ο)	ponos	pain
πόρτα (η)	porta	door
πορτοκάλι (το)	portokalee	orange
πορτοφόλι (το)	portofolee	wallet
πόσα	posa	how many?
πόσο	poso	how much?
πόσο κάνει	poso kanee	how much is it?
πόσο κοστίζει	poso kosteeze	how much does it cost?
ποσότητα (η)	posoteeta	quantity
ποτάμι (το)	potamee	river
πότε;	pote?	when?
ποτέ	pote	never
ποτήρι (το)	poteeree	glass (for drinking)
ποτό (το)	poto	drink

πού;	poo?	where?
πουκάμισο (το)	pookameeso	shirt
πούλμαν (το)	poolman	coach
πουλώ	poolo	to sell
πουρμπουάρ (το)	poorbwar	tip (to waiter, etc)
πούρο (το)	pooro	cigar
πρακτορείο (το)	praktoreeo	agency
πράσινος/η/ο	praseenos/ee/o	green
πρατήριο βενζίνης	prateereeo venzeenees	petrol station
πρατήριο άρτου	prateereeo artoo	baker's
πρεσβεία (η)	presveea	embassy
πριν	preen	before
πρόεδρος (ο)	proedhros	president
προϊόν (το)	proeeon	product
προκαταβολή (η)	prokatavolee	deposit

Greek – English

Greek – English

Greek	Phonetic	English
προορισμός (ο)	pro-oresmos	destination
προπληρώνω (η)	propleerono	to pay in advance
προσγείωση (η)	prosgheeosee	landing
προσδεθείτε	prosdhetheete	fasten safety belts
πρόσκληση (η)	proskleesee	invitation
προσοχή (η)	prosokhee	attention
πρόστιμο (το)	prosteemo	fine
πρωί η (το)	proee	morning
πρωινό (το)	proeeno	breakfast
πρωτεύουσα (η)	protevoosa	capital city
πρώτος/η/ο	protos	first
πρώτες βοήθειες	protes voethee-es	first aid
πρώτη θέση	protee thesee	first class
πρωτοχρονιά (η)	protokhronya	New Years Day

ρP

Greek	Phonetic	English
πτήση (η)	pteesee	flight
πυροσβεστική (η)	peerosvesteekee	fire brigade
πώληση (η)	poleesee	sale
πωλητής/ήτρια(ο/η)	poleetees/eetreea	sales assistant
πώς;	pos?	how?
ρεζέρβα (η)	rezerva	spare wheel
ρεσεψιόν (η)	resepsyon	reception (desk)
ρέστα (τα)	resta	change (money)
ρεύμα (το)	revma	current, electricity
ρόδα (η)	rodha	wheel
ροδάκινο (το)	rodhakeeno	peach
Ρόδος (το)	rodhos	Rhodes (island)
ρολόι (το)	roloee	watch, clock
ρούχα (τα)	rookha	clothes

σΣ

Greek	Transliteration	English
Σαββατοκύ- ριακο (το)	savatokeeryako	weekend
σακάκι (το)	sakakee	jacket (menswear)
σαμπουάν (το)	sambooan	shampoo
σάντουιτς (το)	sandweets	sandwich
σαπούνι (το)	sapoonee	soap
σβήνω	sveeno	to extinguish, to rub out
σέρβις (το)	servees	service (of car etc)
σεφ (ο)	sef	chef
σήμα (το)	seema	sign, signal
σήμερα	seemera	today
στιγά	seegha	slowly
σιδηρόδρομος (ο)	seedheero- dhromos	railway
σιδηροδρομ- ικός σταθμός (ο)	seedheerodhro- meekos stathmos	railway station
σιδηροδρομ- ικώς	seedheerodhro- meekos	by rail
σινεμά (το)	seenema	cinema
σκάλα (η)	skala	ladder, staircase
σκηνή (η)	skeenee	tent, stage
σκι (το)	skee	ski
θαλάσσιο σκι	thalaseeo skee	water-skiing
σκόρδο (ο)	skordho	garlic
σκουπίδια (τα)	skoopeedhya	rubbish, refuse
σκυλί (το)	skeelee	dog
Σκωτία (η)	skotea	Scotland
σκωτσέζικος/ η/ο (η)	skotsezeekos/ ee/o	Scottish (thing)
Σκωτσέζος/ Σκωτσέζα (ο/η)	skotsezos/ skotseza	Scotsman/ Scotswoman
σόμπα (η)	soba	stove, heater
σούπα (η)	soopa	soup
σπανακόπιττα (η)	spanakopeeta	spinach pie
σπίρτο (το)	speerto	match
σπίτι (το)	speetee	house, home

Greek – English

Greek – English

Greek	Pronunciation	English
σπιτικός/ή/ο	speeteekos/ee/o	homemade
σπορ (τα)	spor	sports
Σποράδες (οι)	sporadhes	the Sporades
στάδιο (το)	stadheeo	stadium, stage
σταθμεύω	stathmevo	to park
χώρος σταθμεύσεως	khoros stathmevseos	parking area
σταθμός (ο)	stathmos	station
σιδηροδρο-μικός σταθμός	seedheerodhro-meekos stathmos	railway station
σταθμός υπεραστικών Λεωφορείων	stathmos eeperas-teekon leoforeeon	bus station (intercity)
σταματά!	stamata!	stop!
στάση (η)	stasee	stop
στάση Λεωφορείου	stasee leoforeeo	bus stop
σταυροδρόμι (το)	stavrodhromee	crossroads
σταφύλι (το)	stafeelee	grape
στεγνοκαθα-ριστήριο (το)	steghnokatharee-steereo	dry-cleaner's
στιγμή (η)	steeghmee	moment
συγγνώμη	seeghnomee	sorry, excuse me
συγχαρητήρια	seenkhareeteereea	congratulations
με συγχωρείτε με...	me seenkhoreete me...	excuse me
σύζυγος (ο/η)	seezeeghos	husband/wife
συμπεριλαμ-βάνω	seempereelam-vano	to include
συμπληρώνω	seempleerono	to fill in
σύμπτωμα	seemptoma	symptom
συνάλλαγμα (το)	seenalaghma	foreign exchange
η τιμή του συναλλάγ-ματος	ee teemee too seenalaghmatos	exchange rate
συνάντηση (η)	seenandeesee	meeting

Greek	Transliteration	English
συναντώ	seenando	to meet
συναυλία (η)	seenavleea	concert
συνεργείο (το)	seenergheeo	workshop, garage for car repairs
σύνορα (τα)	seenora	border, frontier
συνταγή (η)	seendaghee	prescription, recipe
συστημένη	seesteemene	recorded
επιστολή (η)	epeestolee	delivery
συχνά	seekhna	often
σχολείο (το)	skholeeo	school (primary)
σώμα (το)	soma	body
σωσίβιο (το)	soseeveeo	life jacket

τ T

ταβέρνα (η)	taverna	tavern with traditional food and wine
ταινία (η)	teneea	film, strip, tape

Greek	Transliteration	English
ταμίας (ο/η)	tameeas	cashier
ταξί (το)	taksee	taxi
αγοραίο ταξί	aghoreo taksee	minicab (no meter)
ράδιο ταξί	radheeo taksee	radio taxi
ταξίδι (το)	takseedhee	journey, tour
καλό ταξίδι	kalo takseedhee	have a good trip
οργανωμένα ταξίδια	orghanomena takseedeea	organised tours
ταξιδιωτικό γραφείο	takseedheeoteeko ghrafeeo	travel agent
ταυτότητα (η)	taftoteeta	identity, identity card
ταχυδρομείο (το)	takheedhromeeo	post office
Ελληνικά Ταχυδρομεία (ΕΛΤΑ)	eleeneeka takheedhromeea	Greek Post Office
ταχύτητα / ταχύτης (η)	takheeteeta / takheetees	speed

Greek – English

Greek – English

Greek	Pronunciation	English
τελευταίος/α/ο	telefteos	last
τέλος (το)	telos	end, tax, duty
οδικά τέλη	odheeka telee	road tax
τέρμα (το)	terma	terminus, end of route
τέχνη (η)	tekhnee	art
λαϊκή τέχνη	laeekee tekhnee	folk art
τζάμι (το)	dzamee	glass (of window)
τζατζίκι (το)	tzatzeekee	tsatsiki (yoghurt, cucumber and garlic)
τηλεκάρτα (η)	teelekarta	phonecard
τηλεόραση (η)	teeleorasee	television
τηλεφώνημα (το)	teelefoneema	telephone call
τηλεφωνικός θάλαμος	teelefoneekos thalamos	phone box
τηλεφωνικός κατάλογος	teelefoneekos kataloghos	telephone directory
τηλεφωνικός κωδικός	teelefoneekos kodheekos	dialling code, area code
τι;	tee?	what?
τι είναι;	tee eenee?	what is it?
τιμή (η)	teemee	price, honour
τιμή εισιτηρίου	eeseeteereeoo teemee	price of ticket, fare
τιμοκατά-λογος (ο)	teemokataloghos	price list
τιμόνι (το)	teemonee	steering wheel
τίποτα	teepota	nothing
τμήμα (το)	tmeema	department, police station
το (with neuter nouns)	to	it, the
τόκος (ο)	tokos	interest (bank)
τοστ (το)	tost	toasted sandwich
τουρισμός (ο)	tooreesmos	tourism
τουρίστας/στρια (ο/η)	tooreestas/streea	tourist

Greek	Pronunciation	English
τουριστικός/ή/ό	tooreesteekos/ee/o	touristic
τουριστικά είδη	tooreesteeka eedhee	souvenirs
τουριστική αστυνομία	tooreesteekee asteenomeea	Tourist Police
Τουρκία (η)	tookeea	Turkey
τραγούδι (το)	traghoodhee	song
τραγωδία (η)	traghodheea	tragedy
τράπεζα (η)	trapeza	bank
τραπεζαρία (η)	trapezareea	dining room
τραπέζι (το)	trapezee	table
τρένο (το)	treno	train
τροχαία (η)	trokhea	traffic police
τροχόσπιτο (το)	trokhospeeto	caravan, mobile home
τρώγω/τρώω	trogho/troo	to eat
τσάι (το)	tsaee	tea
τσάντα (η)	tsanda	bag
τσιγάρο (το)	tseegharo	cigarette
τυρί (το)	teeree	cheese
τυρόπιτα (η)	teeropeeta	cheese pie
τυφλός/ή/ό	teeflos/ee/o	blind
τώρα	tora	now

υΥ

υγεία (η)	eeyeea	health
στην υγειά σας	steen eeyeea sas	your health, cheers
υπηρεσία (η)	eepereseea	service
ποσοστό υπηρεσίας	pososto eepereseeas	service charge
υπόγειος/α/ο	eepoyeeos/a/o	underground
υπόγεια διάβαση πεζών	eepoyeea dheeavasee pezon	pedestrian subway
υπόγειος σι-δηρόδρομος	eepoyeeos see-dheerodhromos	underground (railway)

Greek – English

Greek - English

υπολογιστής (ο)	eepologheestees	computer
υψηλός/η/ό	eepselos/ee/o	high
υψηλή τάση	eepselee tasee	high voltage
ύψος (το)	eepsos	height
ύψος περιορισμένο	eepsos pereeoresmeno	height limit
φ Φ		
φαγητό (το)	fayeeto	food, meal
φαΐ (το)	faee	food
φακός (ο)	fakos	lens, torch
φακοί επαφής	fakee epafees	contact lenses
φακές (οι)	fakes	lentils
φανάρι (το)	fanaree	traffic light, lantern
φαρμακείο (το)	farmakeeo	chemist's
φάρμακο (το)	farmako	medicine
φάω	fao	to eat
φερμπότ (το)	fereebot	ferry boat
φέτα (η)	feta	feta cheese, slice
φιλενάδα (η)	feelenadha	girlfriend
φιλμ (το)	feelm	film
εμφανίσεις φιλμ	emfaneesees feelm	film developing
φίλος/η (ο/η)	feelos/ee	friend
φίλτρο (το)	feeltro	filter
φίλτρο λαδιού	feeltro ladheeo	oil filter
καφές φίλτρου	kafes feeltroo	filter coffee
φλας (ο)	flas	flash (camera), indicators (on car)
φοιτητής/ φοιτήτρια (ο/η)	feeteetees/ feeteetreea	student
φοιτητικό εισιτήριο (το)	feeteeteeko eeseeteereeo	student fare
φόρεμα (το)	forema	dress
φόρος (ο)	foros	tax

φούρνος (o)	foornos	oven, bakery
ΦΠΑ (o)	feepeea	VAT
φρένο (το)	freno	brake (in car)
φρέσκος/ια/ο	freskos/ya/o	fresh
φρούτο (το)	frooto	fruit
φύλακας (o)	feelakas	guard
φύλαξη αποσκευών (η)	feelaksee aposkevon	left-luggage office
φως (το)	fos	light
φωτιά (η)	fotya	fire
φωτογραφία (η)	fotoghrafeea	photograph
φωτογραφίζω	fotoghrafeezo	to take photographs
μη φωτογραφί-ζετε	mi fotoghrafee-zete	no photographs
φωτογραφική μηχανή (η)	fotoghrafeekee meekhanee	camera
φωτοτυπία (η)	fototeepeea	photocopy

χαίρετε	kherete	hello (polite)
χάπι (το)	khapee	pill
χάρτης (o)	khartees	map
οδηκός χάρτης	odheekos khartees	road map
χαρτί (το)	khartee	paper
χαρτί κουζίνας	khartee koozeenas	kitchen paper
χαρτομάντηλο (το)	khartomandeelo	tissue
χαρτονόμισμα (το)	khartonomeesma	banknote
χειροποίητος/η/ο	kheeropee-eetos/ee/o	handmade
χειροτεχνία (η)	kheerotekhneea	handicraft
χειρούργος (o)	kheeroorghos	surgeon
χέρι (το)	kheree	hand, arm
χιλιόμετρο (το)	kheelyometro	kilometre
χιόνι (το)	khyonee	snow
χορός (o)	khoros	dance

Greek – English

Greek – English

Greek	Transliteration	English
χορτοφάγος (ο/η)	khortofaghos	vegetarian
χρειάζομαι	khreeazome	to need
χρήματα (τα)	khreemata	money
χρηματοκι-βώτιο (το)	khreematokeevo-teeo	safe (for valuables)
χρήση (η)	khreesee	use
οδηγίες χρήσεως	odheegheees khreeseos	instructions for use
χρήσιμος/η/ο	khreeseemos/ee/o	useful
χρησιμοποιώ	khreeseemopeeo	to use
Χριστιανός/ή	khreesteeanos/ee	Christian
Χριστούγεννα (τα)	khreestooyena	Christmas
Καλά Χριστούγεννα!	kala khreestooyena	Merry Christmas
χρόνος (ο)	khronos	time, year
χρυσός/ή/ό	khreesos/ee/o	(made of) gold
χρώμα (το)	khroma	colour, paint
χτες	khtes	yesterday
χυμός (ο)	kheemos	juice
χώρα (η)	khora	country
χωριάτικο ψωμί (το)	khoryateeko psomee	bread (round, flat loaf)
χωριό (το)	khoreeo	village
χωρίς	khorees	without
χώρος (ο)	khoros	area, site
αρχαιολογικός χώρος	arkheologheekos khoros	archaeological site
ιδιωτικός χώρος	eedheeoteekos khoros	private land
χώρος σταθμεύσεως	khoros stathmefseos	parking area

ψ Ψ

Greek	Transliteration	English
ψάρεμα (το)	psarema	fishing
ψαρεύω	psarevo	to fish
ψάρι (το)	psaree	fish
ψαρόβαρκα (η)	psarovarka	fishing boat

ψαροταβέρνα (η)	psarotaverna	fish tavern
ψητός/ή/ό	pseetos/ee/o	roasted, grilled
ψυγείο (το)	pseegheeo	fridge, radiator (of car)
ψωμί (το)	psomee	bread

ωΩ

ωτοστόπ (το)	otostop	hitchhiking
ώρα (η)	ora	time, hour
ώρες	ores	visiting hours
επισκέψεως	epeeskepseos	
ώρες	ores	opening hours
λειτουργίας	leetoorgheeas	
της ώρας	tees oras	freshly cooked (food)
ωραίος/α/ο	oreos/a/o	beautiful, nice
ωράριο (το)	orareeo	timetable
ως	os	as, while